CONTENTS

Oppositional Defiant Disorder	v
Introduction	vii
1. My Beloved Child--ODD and Other Behavioral Problems	1
2. Was It Something We Did?	12
3. Your Child Yesterday and Today	25
4. Treatment Strategies for Helping Your Child	33
5. Preventative Measures and Helpful Activities for Children with ODD	50
6. Teaching Strategies for Children with ODD	69
7. Co-Occurring Disorders with ODD	94
8. Oppositional Defiant Disorder in Adults	104
9. Case Studies in ODD	108
Final Words	115
References	119

OPPOSITIONAL DEFIANT DISORDER
THE ULTIMATE PARENTS GUIDE TO CHILDREN AND ADOLESCENTS WITH ODD

S.J. Simmonds

OPPOSITIONAL DEFIANT DISORDER

THE ULTIMATE PARENTS GUIDE TO CHILDREN AND ADOLESCENTS WITH ODD

S.J. SIMMONDS

© Copyright 2019 - All rights reserved.

It is not legal to reproduce, duplicate, or transmit any part of this document in either electronic means or in printed format. Recording of this publication is strictly prohibited and any storage of this document is not allowed unless with written permission from the publisher except for the use of brief quotations in a book review.

INTRODUCTION

In the medical world, Oppositional Defiant Disorder (ODD) is a technical term and scientific description for a type of behavior disorder, diagnosed mostly in children and adolescents. Children with ODD are uncooperative, demanding, hostile towards friends, family and any figure of authority in their lives. Oppositional Defiant Disorder is an exaggerated attempt by children to prove to you that you have no power or authority over them.

Many parents are often left helpless and sometimes in tears thinking about what they could have done wrong. If you are one of those parents, please know that you are not alone. ODD is a serious condition that should be dealt with seriously. There is not a one-size-fits-all solution, and it's not a situation that could be resolved only with medication. Parents of children with ODD should be prepared to not only make drastic changes to and for their children, they should also be prepared to make changes to their entire households and to themselves.

When mental health professionals tell you your child has a disorder, as a parent, all hell breaks loose immediately. The negativity ingrained in the word *disorder* somehow makes you think this disease is somehow your doing as a parent. STOP right there. It is not your fault. You will need to approach this battle in several ways. ODD is not the same for all children. Some children may exhibit extreme behavior more often than others. Some children might be able to express their emotions and what they want but that doesn't mean they are not defiant, while others display this behavior a lot more frequently and intensely than others.

Before you start your battle and read on, it is important to know the difference between Oppositional Defiant Disorder and mental illnesses like schizophrenia, manic depression, or multiple personality disorder. If you have met anyone who is mentally ill with any of those diagnoses, you will be relieved to find out that a person with these kinds of mental illness will likely stay this way more often than anyone with ODD. While you think children with ODD may display very similar behaviors, given the right conditions and circumstances coupled with lovely parents who are always consistent, they quickly change their behavior and grow up to be well-functioning members of society. Do not fret. Take deep breaths now. You are out of the woods. ODD is not a death sentence, after all.

This book will walk you through how to properly set yourself up to help your child. Keep in mind that your patience will be tested but as long as you are aware of the difficulty ahead, giving up is less likely to become an option. Being over-prepared is better than being short-fused when it comes to dealing with children. The more you extend your patience and increase your level of understanding of small things, the better the turnout will be for you.

You will know the different approaches you can use when your child exhibits extreme defiant behavior even for the littlest of things. Even when they start ignoring you, the proper use of reason and logic can convince them to do better. Remember that children think that if they ignore you, they can keep up the guise and continue doing what they want anyway. This book will tell you how to use your words to heal your child and what else you can do when your words fail.

Knowing that you are here, ready to try a positive way to deal with your child's ODD is already reason enough for early congratulations. Many parents struggle with their child's behavior even if undiagnosed yet, and some even resort to violence that sometimes gets out of hand. If you are truly committed to your children like the loving parents that you are, you know that once your child gets the help they need, they will flourish.

The parents' behavior regarding their child's ODD can trigger even more negative reactions and reinforce the child's negative behavior until it becomes a habit for them, so you will need to tread lightly and be mindful of things you do and say. This can affect the way you and your child communicate permanently if you do not begin to follow these steps yourself. As a parent, it is only normal to want the best for your child. You need to extend an even longer layer of patience when battling this disorder, and soon you will yield its fruits that despite your shortcomings, your child does acknowledge authority in their lives and exhibits responsible behavior towards all family and friends.

1

MY BELOVED CHILD--ODD AND OTHER BEHAVIORAL PROBLEMS

*E*very parent feels like their child is perfect. It's difficult to acknowledge that their child's behavior is problematic, and we can't blame them. Having raised them, a parent will always know the quirks of their babies. It could be that they easily get frustrated or immediately throw tantrums when told "No." It can sometimes require a more objective mindset, however, to see if there might actually be a problem. That means you might have to take a step back and assess the situation. You'll have to take off your parent cap to see if your child is really a bit more impulsive than he should be. If you have more than one child, that gives you someone for comparison. If this is your first child, you might watch other children at the playground for comparison or watch the children of your friends to see if your child is frequently and persistently a bit more angry, irritable, argumentative, defiant, and vindictive than other children. It doesn't even have to include all of these behaviors, but perhaps you can recall a time or two that you recognize that your child is a bit more willful than he should be. This is not a diagnosis, this is just to check and observe how your child behaves.

So, what do you look for in your child to see if there is something that you should address? Here are a few characteristics:

Angry and irritable most of the time

- Is your child very touchy and often yells at you or others?
- Is he often violent in his tone even if he is just asking a simple question?
- Does he easily lose his temper with the slightest provocation?

Quarrelsome and defiant

- Does your child immediately blame others for his mistakes?
- Does he deliberately annoy people by repeatedly saying trigger words that often result in escalations?
- Does he actively refuse an adult's request or rule that he already knows?
- Does he get into arguments with adults and teachers or any figure of authority?
- Does he always question the rules?
- Does he outright refuse to follow rules even when you constantly remind him to?

Vindictive

- Is she spiteful in her actions towards you and other people?
- Is the vindictive behavior recurrent?
- Does she speak harshly or unkindly to others?

As a parent, it may be difficult to acknowledge the answers to these questions. If your goal is to help your child and nip the problem in the bud as early as possible, respond with a yes to each question that is true to your child and say it as lovingly as you can. If you have answered YES to some of the questions above, then you have some points to ponder. Make a note, an actual note in a notebook, of when the behavior occurred, what caused it, and how your child expresses the behavior.

If you consistently do this, you can discern patterns as well as triggers that prompt your child's behavior. As parents, we think we know everything about our child including all their triggers and reactions. Without a verified record that you can reference, it can be difficult to discern patterns and easy to forget incidents. So, pick up that pen and make a record. It will help you understand your child better and decide if he or she truly needs help.

What age should I have my child checked for ODD?

Any doctor would wait until the child is at least 4 years old to give a definite diagnosis. A little bit of defiant behavior is normal at ages 2- to 3-years-old. At this stage, children are often overwhelmed with the new world around them and want to use their senses in exploring. They will insist on using all their senses to discover things. This is actually a good thing. It will take more from you as a parent, but putting a little more attention on them during this stage is crucial for their development.

Normal Defiant Behavior

You should allow your child to explore new things to the point of allowing them to find out the consequences of their mistakes. For example, if your child says he doesn't want to put his toys away, you can give him the choice: either he puts them away now or he can do it in 10 minutes. If the defiance continues, you can give him the choice that either he puts them away himself, or you will put them away for him and he won't be allowed to play with them for a week. By following through on your threat, your child will learn that his behavior has consequences.

Research has shown that defiance is part of healthy childhood development. Dix et al. (2007) studied interactions between 119 mothers and their 2- to 3-year-old children. The children were given attractive toys to play with by their mothers. At the end of playtime, the mothers went in to get their children and help them clean up the toys they were given. The reactions of the children were recorded as being defiant, ignoring requests, or compliant.

The results showed that the children of sensitive mothers who had few symptoms of depression were most likely to be defiant, and least likely to ignore their mother's requests. Even in their defiance, however, they initiated positive reactions with their mother. On the other hand, the children of mothers who had symptoms of depression were more likely to ignore requests and less likely to respond with defiance, something researchers described as passive noncompliance. Researchers say that these children develop poorly. They may not have had the chance to develop confident assertions with their mother, learning instead to be overly passive in the face of obstacles.

Their study assures parents that when they first ask children to conform to requests and commands, active resistance is not a sign of problems in childhood development or in relations between parents and children. In fact, at these very young ages, a child's resistance may mean they have developed confidence in their ability to control events and will initiate natural, although immature, attempts to do so (Dix et al., 2007). So, breathe a sigh of relief now. That defiant child of yours is probably normal.

Will my child outgrow this defiant behavior?

In order for your child to outgrow a normal level of oppositional behavior, the child needs to realize that acting out her defiance is not good for her. She needs to know that she is hurting not only herself but others around her. Making a child realize what is right from wrong is quite easy as long as others around her show her the proper way to act. When you constantly show and remind the child how she should behave, she will likely follow your example. You will, however, still need to keep tabs on her defiant behavior as choosing to wait until she outgrows the behavior carries a risk that a problem will go untreated.

If your child's behavior is still concerning at around age 4, it is appropriate at that time to get a diagnosis. It is worth the peace of mind. It's important, however, not to make a big deal out of this to your child. Let him know that you as a family need to find out if he has a condition that requires some help from a doctor to make him feel better. Assure your child that no one but his parents and the doctor will know about any diagnosis that he receives. He doesn't have to tell anyone, and the doctor will help him learn new ways to behave that will ultimately make him happier and healthier.

Is Aggression Contagious?

As parents, we try our best to show love to our kids in everything that we do. One way is to try our best to prevent them from being exposed to aggressive behavior. We know that kids are like sponges and that they absorb anything that they see and hear. We also know that kids are more likely to be aggressive and defiant if exposed to that behavior. So it is our responsibility as parents to make sure that we keep them from anyone who exhibits this behavior, but there might be a place where they might 'catch' that behavior and it might not be somewhere that you expect.

Researchers have studied the effects of behaviors to which children are exposed in the daycare setting. Matlock and Green (1990) explain that daycare contributes to aggression and non-compliance in young children. Specifically, they found that when 4- and 5-year-old children are in daycare, their level of salivary cortisol, a hormone secreted when a person is stressed, is significantly higher than when they are in their own homes with their parents. An increase in cortisol is indicative of an increase in aggression. Matlock and Green (1990) also noted that aggression in daycare-aged children is contagious. When any of the children exhibit aggression, the likelihood that another child will be aggressive increases.

Aggression is particularly contagious if it is successful. This means, if your child sees that one of the children in daycare becomes aggressive in order to get something they want, your child is highly likely to imitate it. Additionally, aggression is likely more contagious if it is exhibited towards another child.

Is this aggression ODD or other possible behavioral problems?

Disruptive Behavior Disorders (DBD) include a broad range of disruptive behaviors. These include both Oppositional Defiant Disorder (ODD) and Conduct Disorder (CD.) Both conditions share the same symptoms, and oftentimes the difference is the severity of the symptom. It is also true that ODD typically progresses to CD as the child ages.

Children with ODD are likely to have more persistent angry, aggressive spurts, arguments and disobedience. Usually they direct their destructive behaviors toward figures of authority like parents and teachers. They may also target their siblings, friends and other children. These behaviors typically last at least six months. For a professional diagnosis, your child will need to have four or more of these symptoms:

- Display aggressiveness more than other children.
- Has consistently shown their aggressive and destructive behavior for at least six months.
- May not have many friends due to their behavior.
- Overall functioning is generally compromised by their challenging behaviors.
- Is angry and resentful most of the time.

- Becomes purposely spiteful and vindictive.
- Argues with adults often.
- Goes out of their way to annoy people.

YOU NEED TO CHECK THAT THESE BEHAVIORS ARE MORE NOTICEABLE IN your child than they are in the other children they play with of the same age; oftentimes, they may not have many children they play with at all.

Conduct Disorder (CD) is a more serious behavior as it includes being aggressive in general towards others and even animals. It is typically diagnosed in older children who show behavior that is destructive to property as well as lying and stealing. They also are more likely to skip school. Children with CD are often labelled as juvenile delinquents. CD is a serious diagnosis and the child should receive professional help from someone the child and the parents trust, someone who can provide a complete, comprehensive evaluation. Children with CD coupled with ADHD, if left untreated, are often doomed to live difficult lives and have significantly poorer outcomes than those with ADHD only.

ATTENTION DEFICIT HYPERACTIVITY DISORDER (ADHD)

Attention Deficit Hyperactivity Disorder (ADHD) is the most common neurodevelopmental disorder in children. The unique thing about ADHD which sets it apart from other DBDs is that it is usually diagnosed first in young children and often lasts into adulthood. If your child has ADHD, it may mean that they may have trouble paying attention. They may sit in class, but are unable to listen. Their minds can be absent from their present location. They may also have trouble with impulsive behaviors. Many children act without thinking about what the consequences of their actions are, while most children with ADHD just are hyperactive.

. . .

OTHER SYMPTOMS OF CHILDREN WITH ADHD

- Often forgetful of where they place their things
- Talk too much
- Cannot control impulses or resist the urge of temptation
- Often cannot get along well with others
- Often absent-minded and daydream a lot
- Squirm or fidget without reason
- Make careless mistakes or take unnecessary risks
- Show trouble with the natural order or taking turns

As you can see, the symptoms of the different DBDs are very similar. A health professional will, however, also require a full examination including a vision test and a hearing test. A Neuropsychiatric EEG-Based Assessment Aid (NEBA) System, a non-invasive scan that measures theta and beta brain waves, is also used along with standard tests. This is part of the complete medical and psychological exam along with a complete medical history to help screen for other particular conditions that may be undiagnosed. Health providers also check for recent life events like:

- Lead poisoning
- Depression
- Anxiety
- Sleep Disorders
- Thyroid Problems
- Undetected or Undiagnosed Seizures

With this information, a health professional can determine if your child has a behavioral disorder. No matter the outcome, it's certain your love for your child won't change. With knowledge, you can now take steps to get your child the treatment he or she needs to develop better behavioral patterns that will lead to a more successful, happier life. To assist in this process, it's a good idea if you can identify the patterns and triggers for the behavior.

IDENTIFYING THE TRIGGERS TO YOUR CHILD'S BEHAVIORS

To discern whether your child has ODD or not, it is important to identify the triggers of your child's behavior. It will take a systematic approach, along with the notes in your notebook, to discover patterns related to your child's behavior. Learning what triggers inappropriate behavior in your child is a big step toward helping your child learn better behavior management skills. When he knows the triggers himself, he will recognize it and use a better approach to how he reacts. This process involves the full commitment of the parents and includes a problem-solving, situational discussion between you and your child. This also takes repetition and time in order to master it, but the good thing is children actually learn it.

Observing and Investigating: When observing your child and looking for patterns, you want to notice the specifics of when they begin acting defiantly, how quickly they resist, if they are angered at reminders, and any details about the behavior itself. If, for example, your child is younger and you notice they act out when you ask them to clean up their toys, observe at which point in the interaction they start acting defiantly towards you. Do they exhibit the defiant behavior immediately? If they happily agree that they will keep their toys picked up after they play and proceed to continue playing, does reminding them to clean it up after they're done set them off? Some children don't like to be disturbed when they are playing, so that may be their trigger.

If they agree that they'll clean it up but then get tired of playing or get distracted and move on to another toy, do they get triggered because you asked them to clean up the toy when they've already moved on? Do they feel like they are pressed to clean as part of play time? Or perhaps it is in the manner of how you remind them. Is your voice raised? Do you constantly remind them and that gets on their nerves? It may take a while, but taking note of these patterns will pay off as you consider whether the behavior is truly indicative of a problem as well as various ways to minimize the behavior.

We all know that raising a child takes a village so you should ask for the help of all the adults who care for your child. Sometimes your child learns not to do the behavior in front of you if they fear your disciplinary response, so you need to enlist the help of others. It may be their teachers or other adults in the household. Tell them that they'll need to find out what happened if your child acted out in defiance in school. You can let them know you are trying to identify the triggers, so they'll know exactly what to look out for. This is especially important if your child is younger and cannot answer adult questions properly. Although this additional step is important, you will still need to find out the situation from your child's point of view and not to judge them even if what they are saying is not in line with what the adults are saying. Let them know you believe what they are saying, and what's more, you want to know what they were feeling and why.

Perception or putting yourself in your child's shoes: Even if you have witnessed the behavior, you should still ask your child's point of view on things. You might have seen them in the act of throwing a toy at their friend, but something else might be happening in their head with regard to what exactly happened. Remember, your child is not evil. They may have been influenced by other things in order to hurt someone on purpose. The goal is to understand why something happened and to know what triggered this behavior in them. Sometimes, if you ask your child about what happened at a later date rather than immediately after something transpired, you may find that they have changed their story. Even these little details can give away why or what they were triggered by. If you have a record of events, that is a valuable document to share with your doctor as he or she tries to discover whether this behavior constitutes an actual behavioral problem or is part of normal defiance.

By learning about these behavioral problems and becoming involved in documenting the patterns of your child's behavior, you'll have a much greater sense of the extent of the problem. It will also help you as you move forward with treatment if your child is diagnosed with a behavioral disorder; if that is the case, don't be discouraged. Your child can learn skills to better control their behavior, and he or she can go on to have a completely normal, healthy, happy life. The key is identifying the problem as early as possible to be able to integrate treatment strategies quickly and effectively. Your child is still your beloved child, so don't lose hope; instead, take action to help them understand their feelings and control their behavior.

CHAPTER SUMMARY

In this chapter, we've discussed the different types of behavioral disorders and the typical symptoms. Specifically, we've discussed the following topics:

- The typical symptoms of a child with behavioral problems
- Normal defiant behavior
- The various disruptive behavioral disorders (DBDs) such as ODD, CB and ADHD
- How to investigate your child's behavior

In the next chapter you will learn about how parenting might affect your child's behavior.

2
WAS IT SOMETHING WE DID?

When you hear that your child has any kind of problem, it's natural to wonder if there was anything you could have done differently to help prevent it. This is particularly true of behavioral disorders since parents tend to feel they must have done something wrong. It's only natural to ask if bad parenting causes ODD.

Did I Do That?

To understand what exactly bad parenting is, we must break down the main categories of parenting:

AUTHORITARIAN PARENTING: This parenting style is an age-old parenting style where a sort of blind obedience from their children is demanded according to very strict tradition. Some characteristics of authoritarian parenting are:

- Parents provide only very limited options for their children

- Parents are emotionally disconnected from or not nurturing to their kids
- Parents do not allow children to express their emotion, or even to challenge their choices and decisions
- Parents punish immediately and sometimes overreact to the slightest mistakes
- Parents expect complete obedience of all their children in the name of tradition or because they were raised the same way
- Parents do not feel the need to explain the rules they set to their children

Research has suggested that the strictest category of parenting, Authoritarian Parenting, has many ill effects on your child. Some of them include:

- Poor and disconnected social skills
- Absent or very poor self-esteem or self-confidence
- Increased likelihood to develop depression in adulthood

It might be time to step back and check if you are an authoritarian parent. Many times the authoritarian parent doesn't know what they are doing is wrong. They have the best intentions, thinking it is the way to ensure their children do their best in school, or they feel that they have been raised this way and they turned out fine. Sometimes, punishment involving yelling is used, and this will certainly cause more violent behaviors to be exhibited by the child into adulthood. Try to reassess your actions as a parent and be more considerate towards your child or children, especially if they are still very young.

AUTHORITATIVE PARENTING: THIS PARENTING STYLE USES A SYSTEM OF positive reinforcement and reasoning. Authoritative parents, unlike Authoritarian ones, are sensitive to their child's needs and are generally warm and affectionate. This style of parenting is common throughout the world in educated and middle-income parents, and it is associated with superior child outcomes throughout the world. Some characteristics of authoritative parents are:

- Parents respect their child's opinions and encourage them to express themselves
- Parents explain and provide reason for the rules that they set
- Parents help the child emotionally when they are scared or upset
- Parents try their best to learn about their child's emotions and listen to them
- Parents consider the child's choices before they ask them to do something

The common characteristics of children with authoritative parenting are:

- The children feel more secure as they know they can count on their parents when they are overwhelmed.
- Children of authoritative parents are less likely to develop drug addiction and alcohol use in adulthood.
- Children are perceptive to emotional cues and are sensitive to the behaviors of others around them.
- They are less likely to be aggressive and have less problems with their peers in school.

So what exactly is authoritative parenting? If you are not clear on its definition yet, imagine you are a mother lioness. You love your children with all your heart, and you set some boundaries for them. You let them pick what they want within your boundaries of control that you know they are safe with, but they have enough freedom knowing they can choose. You inspire positive feelings in your children and give them warmth and love, but at the same time, just like the lioness that you are, you encourage your child's sense of autonomy and instill a sense of self-discipline and maturity. You allow your kids to make mistakes and to learn from these mistakes because you put so much energy into the development of your child. In short, you are highly demanding because you know that they can do it. This is why authoritative parents are also strict but in ways that are very different from authoritarian parents.

PERMISSIVE PARENTING: THIS STYLE OF PARENTING DOESN'T INVOLVE disciplining your child. You fulfill your role as a parent by loving and nurturing them, but without discipline. This style can easily backfire. If you are a permissive parent, you do not assign your kids any responsibilities, nor do you set behavior standards or models for them to follow. Permissive parenting is similar to treating your child as your friend and allowing them to treat you as a friend. This frequently results in a tendency for the child to be manipulative to get what they want. There are some similarities between permissive parenting to authoritative parenting because they are both warm and nurturing to their children, but they are very different in other ways. Permissive parenting traits include:

- Permissive parents generally ignore their child's bad behavior
- They give in to the child when they are throwing a temper tantrum
- They resolve all their child's problems so the child will not encounter any difficulty

Children of permissive parents are usually characterized by the following traits:

- Demanding and have difficulty sharing
- Do not take responsibility for their behavior
- Lack overall general discipline

- Refuses to follow authority
- Have little to no self-control

Although it is unimaginable to not set discipline standards for your children, this approach is more common than we think. There are some benefits to permissive parenting. First, you are highly nurturing and loving to the point that you make your children's happiness your priority above all else. Sometimes, this is a result of your own unhappy childhood, and you don't want your child to experience the same kind of difficulty you had when you were a child. That isn't necessarily bad, of course, but it is not without its consequences.

This kind of parenting is also the one with the least arguments or no arguments at all. You do not want to upset your child so you give in to your child's demands. Your relationship is generally peaceful. Also, permissive parenting is where your child can explore their true creativity. Since you place no limitation, the child can unleash their latent creativity. The lack of discipline, however, often results in children who have a sense of entitlement, and that causes problems as they mature.

Uninvolved Parenting: There is a fourth category of parenting which is the uninvolved parent. From the name itself, you are not involved in your child's life except for providing the basics of food, clothing and shelter. This is usually not a style of parenting that one often chooses, and in fact, most of the time parents who follow this kind of parenting style are doing so unintentionally, so we should not immediately pass judgment. For example, a parent who is dealing with their own issues may be unable to be involved in their child's life to any greater extent. Characteristics of parents who follow this parenting style:

- They focus only on their own problems and desires.

- They are not capable of emotional attachment, by choice or not.
- They lack interest in their children's daily activities
- They do not set expectations of or appropriate levels of behavior for their children

Clearly, this kind of style can result in children with numerous behavioral problems, but we won't delve further into this style as this is probably not something you would choose as a type of parenting style. Instead, it's a style that mostly likely occurs due to the circumstances created from your life.

Bad Parenting as a Cause of ODD

While there is some truth that ODD is associated with absent or neglectful parenting, children with loving and present parents also develop the condition. Research hasn't determined a clear cause of ODD, but it is more than just your choice of parenting style. Some children are probably genetically predisposed to the condition, making them more likely to develop ODD as compared to other children.

Other mental health conditions and developmental issues are also contributing factors. We'll discuss later those conditions which tend to co-occur with ODD. The reactions from the different people your child interacts with can also affect whether their behavior gets better or becomes worse. This being said, a careful balance of freedom, a sense of autonomy within boundaries, is the best kind of parenting, and it is more than the labels that are put on these parenting styles. We always try to adjust our parenting style to what our child needs at the moment, and what we think is best for them. To know what's best, it's also important to understand both the heritable (i.e. inherited) and the environmental causes that play a role in this disorder.

. . .

HERITABILITY OF ODD

There are a number of studies that indicate a high heritability with ODD as well as many other disruptive behavioral disorders. It's useful at this point to discuss a little about how genetic heritability is researched. Heritability quite simply refers to the degree to which your genes are affecting a physical trait or behavioral outcome. Of course, we've known for many years that your physical features are genetically influenced. More recently, research has focused on the heritability of behaviors. Usually, these studies involve the use of identical twins.

Identical twins, also called monozygotic twins, result from the fertilization of a single egg which then splits and becomes two individuals. With the exception of some mutations, these twins share identical DNA. This is compared to dizygotic twins who result from the fertilization of two eggs. This fertilization occurs at the same time, and the resulting fetuses gestate together, but they are no more closely related than any other siblings. They don't share identical DNA.

The reason it's useful to involve identical twins in these types of studies is because they share identical DNA. If a trait is strongly under genetic control, then both twins should exhibit that trait, whether it's behavioral or physical. Researchers can measure the degree to which identical twins do share physical and/or behavioral traits, and that then allows them to understand the genetic influences on the trait as well as how big of a role the external environment and individual psychological makeup play in the expression of that trait.

For example, if researchers discover that 35 percent of the variation in a particular behavioral trait can be explained by genetics, that means 65 percent is explained by non-genetic, environmental factors or individual psychological factors. It's important here to understand that environmental factors include such things as your child's nutritional environment, his physical environment, the parenting strategies to which he is exposed, the socioeconomic status of his family, and those experiences he has with other children and adults as well as any other non-genetic factors.

To further determine the role of genetics versus environmental factors, researchers will use identical twins who were raised in the same home and compare them to identical twins not raised in the same home and dizygotic twins (non-identical twins), both those who were raised together and those who apart. The expectation would be that if a trait is highly heritable, i.e. strongly under genetic control, then the identical twins will share the trait regardless of whether they are raised together or not, and they will share the trait much more frequently than dizygotic twins, both those raised together and those raised apart.

For ODD, researchers would examine identical twins and record the variation they see with whether or not both twins demonstrate the behavioral disorder. They would look at how many sets of twins share the trait regardless of whether they were raised together or not as well as how many dizygotic sets of twins share the trait.

One such study (Mikolajewski et al., 2017) found a moderate to high heritability for ODD (between 24 and 63 percent) with regard to what the researchers described as headstrong/hurtful behaviors and irritability behaviors. They also found that ODD in childhood poses a significant risk for certain mental health problems in late adolescence. These problems include substance abuse, antisocial behaviors and overall externalizing behaviors. The latter refers to acting out against others when they feel frustrated.

Another study (de Zeeuw et al., 2015) found a similar heritability for ODD (around 50 percent), but found that a shared classroom experience had a significant effect on the behaviors as well. The researchers also noted that parental discipline and a level of involvement in their children's lives were significant contributors to the expression of the behaviors associated with ODD. This was more true for ODD than it was for ADHD, which showed a stronger genetic influence. Given this, it's also important to examine the environmental causes of ODD.

ENVIRONMENTAL CAUSES OF ODD

We've discussed the role that parenting styles play in behavioral problems in children, and that is one environmental factor associated with ODD. But, there are many others, so let's delve a little more deeply into some external factors that could potentially cause ODD in your child. Take note that untreated ODD greatly increases the risk for substance abuse and juvenile delinquency when they become older (Mikolajewski et al., 2017).

Recent studies show that up to 15% of school children are diagnosed with either ADHD, ODD, or CD. This likely means that a good percentage of children live in stressed and frustrated families. Because of their complicated and stressful situations, these children are very hard to isolate and understand individually, but there are definitely patterns suggesting significant environmental influence on the development of ODD.

Prenatal Factors and Childbirth Complications

While you might not think of it this way, the prenatal environment is just that, an environment. It's not your child's genetics, it is the environment in which they are developing. Thus, problems while the child is inside the mother's body are potential environmental contributors to behavioral disorders such as ODD. One study (Gump et al., 2017) found that factors affecting the prenatal environment like lead poisoning and protein deficiency placed the child at a higher risk of developing ODD. Several other studies (Bada et al., 2007; Linares et al., 2005; Spears et al., 2010) have shown that a mother's use of alcohol or drugs during pregnancy can result in an increased risk for a child developing ODD. That's because these substances change the intrauterine environment, and that has a direct effect on the developing child.

Neurobiological Factors

Developmental differences and physical injuries to an area of the brain can also lead to behavioral problems, and it constitutes a contributing environmental factor. Studies that involved taking images of the brain have shown that children with ODD might have some subtle differences with regard to their reasoning, judgment and impulse control. More specifically, they're believed to have an overactive behavioral activation system which is the part of the brain that generates behavior in response to a reward or lack of punishment. They also have an underactive behavioral inhibition system, which is that part of the brain responsible for generating anxiety and limiting ongoing behaviors that are happening in the presence of either a new experience, a fear stimulus, or signals of punishment (Matthys et al., 2012).

Additionally, research has identified some structural and functional differences in several regions of the brain in children with conduct disorders. The areas affected include the amygdala, prefrontal cortex, anterior cingulate and insula. There are some interconnected regions that show differences, too (Matthys et al., 2012). While some developmental differences may be caused by genetic factors, these can also result from injuries caused by exposures to toxins like alcohol or drugs in utero, infection, or an actual physical injury (Queensland Brain Institute, 2020).

Socio-cognitive Factors

Children who suffer from conduct problems often exhibit significant socio-cognitive impairments. In fact, as much as 40 percent of boys and 25 percent of girls with disruptive behavioral disorders show these kinds of impairments. They take the form of immature forms of thinking like egocentrism, cognitive distortion like interpreting a neutral act as hostile, and a failure to use verbal mediators to regulate their own behavior (Mash & Wolfe, 2012). Moreover, children with ODD are limited with respect to their social knowledge, and that is a factor in how they are able to process information and cognitively address problems. That often results in difficulty controlling their emotions and behavior (Goldstein & DeVries, 2017).

The social information processing model (SIP) states that children go through five stages before actually engaging in a behavior. These include encoding, mental representations, response accessing, evaluation, and finally, enactment. Children with ODD, however, experience cognitive distortions that impair their ability to process social information. That typically results in a negative impact on their interactions and relationships, particularly among their peers. They often experience a loss of friendships and interruptions in those activities that are socially engaging. Additionally, since children learn through observation and social modeling, impairments can greatly affect their ability in this regard (Goldstein & DeVries, 2017).

OTHER ENVIRONMENTAL FACTORS

As previously described, negative parenting and conflict between the child and one or more parents frequently leads to antisocial behavior. In families where there is a history of substance abuse or mental illness that has led to dysfunctional interactions and/or inconsistency in discipline can result in DBD. Moreover, in families where there is a failure on the part of the parents to help the child adjust to changing situations, the child is at higher risk for ODD (Goldstein & DeVries, 2017). Other familial factors for the development of ODD include things like a weak parent-child attachment, a lack of internalization of both parental and societal standards on the part of the child, low socioeconomic status, a lack of supervision and living in high-risk neighborhoods where the child is exposed to violence (Eiden et al., 2014; Vanfossen et al., 2010; White & Renk, 2011).

COMORBIDITIES

We'll discuss comorbidities in more detail in a subsequent chapter, but suffice it to say that researchers have also noted that children with behavior disorders are often found to have comorbidities, even if each one has different external factors growing up. These external factors include inattention, hyperactivity, aggression and defiance. What scientists do not yet know, however, is why these children with comorbidities have behavior disorders that go along with it. To date, the genetic and environmental etiology that underlies the comorbidity among these disruptive behavior disorders is unclear. Scientists have also found out that children with diagnosed ODD are at a higher risk for later substance use and dependence.

Although quite distinct from each other, studies have shown that ODD is a precursor to CD, and older children diagnosed with CD are more apt to develop other psychiatric disorders when they become adults, including antisocial personality disorder. Evidence shows that children who have these disruptive behaviors often come from dysfunctional families, have been exposed to ill-behaving parents with alcoholism or marital conflicts, or have parents who had been abused or neglected themselves. If children have the genetic factors that make them predisposed to disruptive behaviors and are subsequently exposed environmentally, they will most likely develop either ADHD, ODD or CD or even a combination of these disruptive behaviors and the effects last well into adulthood (Noordermeer et al., 2017).

Research (Boylan et al., 2007) has also shown that children with ODD frequently demonstrate comorbidity with anxiety and depression. These types of problems are identified as internalizing disorders because, rather than acting outwardly aggressive toward other children or adults, these children turn the destruction inward. This research also shows that internalizing comorbidities are present in all age groups and appear to be more of a problem in children who develop ODD early in life.

It should be clear at this point that the etiology behind ODD and other behavioral disorders is complex. There are genetic factors as well as environmental factors that play a role in whether your child could develop one of these behavioral problems. In fact, it's likely a mix of the two: a child is born with the genes that predispose the child to the problem, but it isn't until they are exposed to certain environmental factors that they actually develop the disorder. Those environmental factors can include parenting styles, but they certainly aren't the only environmental factors that can cause a behavioral disorder. As a parent, you'll likely want to try to do anything you can to prevent your child from experiencing these problems. What you can do is to check your parenting style and ideally try to develop an authoritative style. The child's environment needs reasonable discipline, but with freedom to explore, as well, to help your child develop the skills necessary for them to regulate their own behavior.

Chapter Summary

In this chapter, we've discussed the various causes for ODD and other behavioral disorders. Specifically, we've discussed the following topics:

- The various parenting styles and their effect on children's behavior.
- The heritability--or genetic contribution--of ODD.
- Environmental contributions to the development of ODD.

In the next chapter, you'll discover the ways in which the differences in your child's brain can affect their behavior.

3

YOUR CHILD YESTERDAY AND TODAY

*I*t is only natural for a parent to want to take extra measures to understand their child's behavior. Understanding how your child perceives things by asking them what happened, as we suggested in our previous chapter, is definitely a big help in this journey. Now, we'll need to understand what causes your child's brain to be the way it is. Understanding the science behind what is going on in their brains will help you help your child cope with their feelings and manage the way they respond to their triggers.

FEAR AND PUNISHMENT

Children with ODD or symptoms of ODD are thought to react to physical stimuli such as fear and punishment differently from kids who don't exhibit symptoms of defiant behavior. Researchers have observed changes in cortisol activity levels in the brains of children with ODD when reacting to stress, and they also show an abnormal level of serotonin and noradrenaline. This means that punishment and fear are likely to have a different effect on them. The difference in brain activity means that they feel different and respond differently, and therefore the negative effects are different as well. Typically, these differences will cause children with ODD to be less responsive to rewards and less fearful of punishment, which causes them to act out more impulsively.

Underdeveloped Prefrontal Cortex

Research also shows that the prefrontal cortex, which is the part of the brain that controls impulsive behavior, is believed to be underdeveloped in children with ODD. The prefrontal cortex is responsible for managing executive functions like emotional behavior and impulsivity. This means that your child may be biologically unable to manage control of their impulse which then results in erratic bursts of behavior. It might be possible to use certain techniques to help them with managing their impulses, but it is something that will take practice for them to learn. The prefrontal cortex development starts early in life and continues until we are well into our mid 20s or later. That is why some kids do grow out of the defiant behavior but some take longer than others to do so.

Impulse Control Disorders

Having an underdeveloped prefrontal cortex can cause other disorders aside from ODD. It is worth looking into so you understand all the potential effects it may have on your child. If you suspect that your child may have one or more of these disorders, please contact your mental health provider immediately to assess the situation. Impulse control disorders are quite common and can be destructive and debilitating for adults and much more so for children. Some of these disorders include:

- ODD
- Intermittent Explosive Disorder
- Conduct Disorder
- Antisocial personality
- Pyromania

- Kleptomania

In a nutshell, they are called Impulse Control Disorders because these are caused by the underdeveloped prefrontal cortex, and therefore, the child or adult cannot help these behaviors. ODD is usually diagnosed in children and is defined as defiant behavior towards adults or any person of authority. Conduct Disorder is repetitive aggression behavior towards others that may involve abuse and physical destruction of property. Intermittent Explosive Disorder (IED) is defined by repeated, destructive, uncontrollable temper tantrums mostly by adults, and antisocial personality is total disregard for the feelings and safety of others around you. What links these conditions together is the compulsive need to engage in harmful and threatening behaviors not only towards themselves but to others as well. They are also referred to as behavioral addictions because the individual experiences sensations similar to addicts, including feelings of compulsion, craving, loss of control, and hedonistic release or pleasure seeking behaviors, which is the actual characteristic of addiction.

There are also documented physical changes that can be measured in individuals suffering from impulse control disorders. Glutamine, an important amino acid with many functions in the body, is present where it is usually not, and that is combined with dopamine, a type of neurotransmitter involved in sending messages between nerve cells. Dopamine plays a big part in how we feel about pleasure and our ability to think and plan ahead. When both are present in a given situation, it essentially makes our willpower useless. Moreover, MRI scans in children with ODD demonstrate scattered cortical and subcortical regions becoming active when they are faced with a stimulus for their impulse. Another region affected, the frontal pole, is the part of the brain that controls impulsivity, and research also shows this area is underactive in children with ODD. Therefore, the deck is stacked against them for being able to control their behavior. It takes a lot of unconditional love to help them gain control.

. . .

A Mother's Unconditional Love--One Woman's Story

In the book, *The Whipped Parent: Hope for Parents Raising an Out-of-Control Teen*, Kim Abraham details her powerful journey involving her son Nathan who has been dealing with ODD since he was a child. As a child, Nathan would refuse to go to school which forced Kim to drag him out of bed and into the car in his pajamas. Nathan would also steal things from his brother and break his father's tools. His parents had to lock everything up to ensure he didn't get to them, but he'd learned how to break into things to get what he wanted. When he was in middle school, he refused to wear clean clothes for weeks and opted instead for the dirtiest and most ragged clothes he could find. Nathan's behavior created never-ending problems with his parents. Kim remembers crying and asking Nathan, "Why are you doing this to me?" It's such an incredibly difficult and frustrating experience. There is, however, hope for anyone in this situation.

When you find yourself doubting your judgment and experiencing uncontrollable frustration, please make sure to seek help. Any parent would be sucked into that cycle and it takes a lot to step back and assess how you will handle the situation. Many times, professional help is not easily accessible, but you can reach out to your local mental health center or a friend for some support. Kim had thought of Nathan as her most difficult child. She had done everything to try and find something he would be interested in with the hope that she would find the one thing that would set him straight. He was bouncing from activity to activity, and he would lose interest quickly. He was already 14-years-old when he was officially diagnosed with ODD. The doctor wasn't concerned because he was only looking out for ADHD, so her concerns were dismissed. Nathan's ODD was ruining her life. She said that his behavior has taken away any feeling of any kind of empowerment as a parent. "That's a terrible feeling. That's when you get really angry."

After the initial diagnosis, Kim spent time with a slew of therapists with Nathan. The first professional told her, after just one session, that kids like hers would usually end up in an institution even if they had intensive therapy. She definitely didn't go back to him. The second therapist thought she needed to improve her parenting skills saying Nathan needed a consistent parent who could implement consistent consequences. Kim knew, however, that she was already consistent. Every time Nathan did something he was told not to, she followed every rule in the book, every piece of advice from previous doctors and parents, but the problem was that Nathan just didn't care. She would ground him but he would just look at her and insist that he was not and just walk out the door. It reached a point where if Kim took something from him as a punishment, he would break into his parents' bedroom to take it back. He would leave his Dad's tools lying around or lose them, so his Dad had to lock their garage but Nathan would break in and resume his misdeeds. That's when Kim realized that traditional discipline doesn't work for kids like Nathan. She realized that while therapists emphasize consequences for kids like Nathan, she knew that it was better to focus on the positive side of things like rewarding good behavior, refusing to engage in arguments, and building self-esteem. She also designed a good method, her own system, that worked with Nathan where she felt she was 100% in control. It was her system of reciprocity.

Whenever she would ask Nathan to do something and he refused, she would also turn down his next request. For example, if Nathan asked for a ride to a friend's house, she would refuse letting him know that she would love to do it but he needed to reciprocate the favor. It took a while before it dawned on him, but eventually Nathan got tired of being refused and he learned that he should pull his own weight in their home. Finally, Nathan was learning that relationships are a two-way street. Kim said she was prepared to see her new method through to the end even if it didn't click with Nathan. It was the real world, and he needs to know that if you don't do something for someone, then you don't get what you want back. Nathan did eventually learn and improve his behavior. There were many drawbacks and relapses along the way, but Kim is happy to share that Nathan did improve drastically. He is now an adult with a successful business. He even has kids of his own. Nathan has indeed come far, but not without the constant efforts from his family, and most especially his mother.

What you can take away from this story is that it is possible to love your child unconditionally. Sometimes, you can say things that seem hurtful and that proves you are just as human as anyone else. In truth, every child has their own challenges. There will always be the need to assess how to handle each situation. The goal is to help them become productive, independent individuals who can engage in healthy relationships. Kim's story shows that despite getting minimal help from health professionals, parents can develop strategies for helping their children overcome the challenges of a behavioral disorder. The key to doing that is noticing those patterns. Kim saw that traditional punishments weren't working with Nathan, and she developed a different strategy involving reciprocal rewards. Your child might respond better to those traditional disciplinary actions or he may need a mixed approach. Still, with persistence and consistency, you can develop a strategy that will help you and your child have a happier experience while they are young.

Working with a child who has behavioral disorders can be a tall order, and it will definitely leave you feeling frustrated and exhausted much of the time. It's important, however, that you maintain your cool. Here are some concrete steps you can turn to when you feel a little frustrated or exhausted:

1. **Be the example.** It may be tough but knowing that your child is a sponge and absorbs everything that he sees and more can motivate you to be the example your child needs you to be. He will look back on his life and know that his parents tried their best, and he will one day be the example for his child, too. Regulate the attitude that you show your child. Many of the things he acquires are from his environment and most especially from his mother.
2. **Ask for help.** Asking for help is exhausting, especially if you've done it a few times, but don't stop asking. The

burden is a lot easier to carry if you don't do it alone. There are many support groups out there, and you will find one where you belong. Even finding one that you could vent to is a great help. Having friends and family to reach out to is fantastic, but for some reason we always share and feel connected more to strangers, especially if they are going through the same thing we are.

3. **Make time for your child.** Yes, we spend hours on end everyday with our child arranging playdates, creating fun activities or traveling, but make the effort to make extra time when you are not stressed out about the activities you are planning. Take this time to just reach out and bond with your child and be more spontaneous. Routine is great for children, but spontaneity is good for Mom. Your child will be happy to know that you are available for them. Winning the heart of your child requires time and much more if you've gone through a tumultuous journey involving therapist after therapist with them. This is a good time for extra affection, cuddles, tickles and smiles. If they know they can get hugs and cuddles from Mom, they'll know that there are also good days.

4. **Celebrate small wins.** It's exhausting battling with ODD every day, so take what you can and celebrate the small milestones with your child. Give lots of encouragement and praise. This reassures them that despite their negative behavior, their parents continue to love them, and that gives your child reason to be better every day. Show your child the small tasks they can do themselves so they too can celebrate small wins. Letting them know that you are both on a journey and sharing the load will make it so much easier. Praise them when they read a book by themselves quietly or pick up an item that they threw around earlier. It'll come naturally for them eventually.

5. **Enrich their spirituality.** If you are religious, pray together with your child. If you are not, let them realize

that they have an inner self that they are protecting. The inner self is the one that doesn't get in trouble with teachers and isn't as messy. Teach them that if they are sad or mad, they can turn to their spiritual beliefs and know that there is a presence they can turn to without being judged. Many times, when children have that sense of belief, they are helping to uncover things about themselves which they don't know, and that helps with their development.

By keeping your cool and staying consistent, calm and collected even when your child acts out, you'll be much more able to manage the situation. It's important to remember how their brain is responding to the situation. It's also important to take care of yourself so you'll have the energy to meet the challenges that lie ahead.

Chapter Summary

In this chapter, we've talked about what's going on from your child's perspective. Specifically, we've talked about the following topics:

- How your child's brain perceives fear and punishment.
- What areas of the brain are affected by behavior disorders like ODD.
- How unconditional love can lead to a better understanding and more effective treatments for your child.
- The importance of taking care of yourself.

In the next chapter you will learn about treatment strategies for helping your child manage ODD.

4
TREATMENT STRATEGIES FOR HELPING YOUR CHILD

With a good basic understanding of the causes of ODD, the various behaviors involved and what is happening physically in the brain, it's helpful to examine what is typically done to formally diagnose ODD and the treatment options available to children and families. The quicker you are able to respond to what you see as disruptive behavior, the better the chances your child can learn to manage the behavior for a healthier, happier life. So, what does it take to get the disorder diagnosed?

Diagnosis of ODD

We've already discussed the symptoms of ODD, including aggressive, defiant behavior and an argumentative attitude toward other children and adults. When you decide it's time to seek professional help, what will happen?

Normally, once you notice what you identify as definitive symptoms of a problem, you can seek a diagnosis from a child psychiatrist or other qualified mental health expert. As mentioned earlier, experts are unwilling to render a diagnosis until the child is at least 4 years of age since defiant behavior is commonplace in children experiencing the terrible twos (and threes). If your child is 4-years-old or older, however, you can seek a diagnosis. This is where it is extremely important to bring your notebooks with the patterns of behavior you have observed.

To diagnose your child with ODD, mental health experts will want to see any evidence you've gathered, they will want to talk with both parents as well as the child's teachers or any other caregivers who are around the child consistently. They might also want to observe the child for themselves, and they could want to conduct other mental health tests to be certain it's ODD versus some other condition and to identify comorbidities.

It is necessary for a diagnosis to show that the child has been experiencing persistent symptoms for at least six months. This is where those notebooks will come in handy. There is no single test that can be used to diagnose this condition, and thus, the mental health professional must rely on assessing the symptoms and behavior they see in the child. Most parents begin by taking the child to their general physician, and that's also where you will begin the process of documenting a medical history. Your GP will also want to perform a physical examination to rule out any physical medical ailments. Then, typically, the GP will refer the child to a mental health professional trained to work with children and adolescents.

The mental health professional will gather information from you, teachers, daycare providers and any other caregivers who have knowledge of the child's behavioral patterns. The more people who can help you document the behavior, the better. That yields more information about the patterns and triggers that set your child off. Once the expert has gathered the data they need, they can assess a number of factors. They can determine if the behavior is severe, with whom and when the behavior occurs, and any stressful situations within the home. This helps the mental health professional to determine if the child indeed has ODD or if they might just be responding to some kind of short-lived stressor.

The professionals will often make use of rating scales and questionnaires to determine the severity of the behaviors. Not only will these tools help with diagnosis, they will also help to monitor the progress of treatment. Your mental health professional will also look for any signs of other conditions that typically co-occur with ODD like ADHD, anxiety, depression, or other mood disorders. One sign that the doctor should be sure to look for is bullying--either as victim or perpetrator--since this is a big, red flag that your child is at risk for aggressive, impulsive behavior.

TREATMENT OPTIONS

Since there are no one-size-fits-all treatment options for children and teens with ODD, the treatment plans that are most effective are those that are tailored to the specific needs and symptoms of each child. Your medical expert will determine the best treatment plan depending on the severity of the behaviors and if there are any co-occurring mental health conditions. It's also important for the mental health professional to consider the goals and circumstances of the child's parents as they formulate a treatment plan. The plan will require the commitment and follow-through of the parents and any other caregivers in consistent contact with the child, and it may take several months before you begin to see real progress. While treatment plans are individualized, there are some typical combinations:

Cognitive Problem-Solving Skills Training: This type of training works to reduce the inappropriate behaviors by instructing the child in more positive ways to respond to those stressful situations. Many children with ODD simply don't know a better way to interpret and respond to the situations in which they feel triggered. This training shows them different and healthier ways to handle those situations. Most behavioral interventions usually begin by conducting a behavioral analysis. This is where both positive and negative behaviors are selected as behaviors to either increase or decrease using a well-structured plan that includes such things as alternative ways to handle situations where the child is triggered, immediate incentives to increase a desired behavior, and consequences designed to decrease a negative behavior (Villodas et al., 2012).

When the contingency behaviors are implemented immediately in response to a situation where the child is triggered, they work better to help resolve the problems. The research has shown that children with ODD do respond well to partial or delayed reinforcement. It also helps if parents give clear, effective instructions and implement a well-structured routine that includes consistent rules and expectations as well as rewards for positive behavioral responses. The system put in place should also be coordinated with the child's school (Villodas et al., 2012).

Anger Management Training: Children with ODD often have specific problems controlling their anger. This type of training can teach them relaxation techniques to help them more effectively manage feelings of anger. It also often includes training in setting goals, identifying triggers and recognizing potential consequences for their actions.

Socials Skills Training: Many people with ODD have problems with resolving social challenges such as a fight with a friend. This type of training can help them to master social skills that will support healthier relationships. It can also help to prevent problems from occurring in school or at work.

School-Based Programs: These kinds of programs help teach children and teens ways they can relate more positively to their peers as well as ways to improve in their schoolwork. These kinds of therapies are more effective if they can be conducted in a natural environment, meaning the school itself or within a social group.

Play Therapy: While adults can have ODD, it is much more common in children. Young children may have difficulty understanding other types of therapy or with expressing their emotions. Play therapy is a great way to help them with that. They can work out their emotions which will help them to understand their own behavior and master healthier coping skills.

Medication: Sometimes medication may be necessary to help control the more challenging symptoms of ODD, particularly if there are coexisting conditions like ADHD, anxiety or mood disorders. Even if medication is used as a treatment, it should not be the only treatment implemented. Medication should only be used as part of a more comprehensive plan that helps both parents and children control specific behaviors as well as treat any co-occurring conditions. Often, medication for a co-occurring condition may, in fact, lessen the symptoms of ODD as well. This is true, for example, when ODD and ADHD coexist. If the coexisting condition is a mood disorder or anxiety, it may be prudent to treat the child with antidepressants and anti-anxiety medications. When used properly, medication can be an effective adjunct to a more comprehensive treatment plan.

TREATMENTS ACCORDING TO AGE GROUPS

Treatment also varies according to the age group of the child. For preschool-age children, the treatment plan will often focus on parent-management training and education. Those children who are school-age, however, perform better with a combination of the parent management training, individual therapy and various school-based interventions. Adolescents also benefit most when parent management training is implemented. Individual therapy that focuses on helping the child develop problem-solving skills is also helpful in all age groups. It can greatly improve problematic behaviors in children and adolescents with ODD. The kinds of problem-solving skills taught should be those that are tailored to the child's specific behavioral problems, and of course, they should be appropriate for the child's age. This therapy should focus on helping the child acquire new skills since the ones with which they are familiar are not working.

Peer Group Therapy: This therapy involves putting your child in a therapy group with peers suffering from the same problems. They can see that they are not the only ones with this type of problem, and peers often have helpful strategies that children are more likely to appreciate and use. Sometimes, they can come to see their parents as too authoritarian, particularly if your child is an adolescent. Peers, on the other hand, are less threatening, and if they are also going through the same kind of problem, they can understand your child's perspective even better than you can.

Multi-Component Implementations: There are several types of behavioral interventions that have been used to help manage behavioral problems in children with persistent aggressive conduct problems. Two such interventions are behavioral parent training (BPT) and behavioral classroom management (BCM). These have been used successfully individually and in combination. They're particularly helpful for children who develop problems early in life since they require more intensive strategies that are coordinated across multiple contexts. By using a multiple component approach, it is even possible to treat youth who suffer from both ADHD and ODD or CD. Here are some examples of multi-component programs available to help your child:

Incredible Years

One multi-component implementation that has been quite successful is called *Incredible Years*. It's a comprehensive intervention for multiple settings that was developed for children between the ages of 3- and 7-years-old. This program integrates child skills training interventions with BPT and BCM. By combining the interventions, the program can help children who suffer from both ADHD and ODD. In fact, a randomized trial carried out over 20 weeks showed moderate improvement for children demonstrating externalizing behavior (meaning they were directing their aggression outward rather than inward). The children also showed moderate to marked improvement for problems related to inattention, hyperactivity, aggression and defiance, particularly with parents.

First Steps to Success

Another multi-component intervention program, called *First Steps to Success*, is helpful for children in Kindergarten through the third grade with ODD or CD. This program, like *Incredible Years*, utilizes both BPT and BCM components and consists of 30 program days during which the interventions are implemented at school and six sessions implemented in the home. The home sessions help parents learn the strategies to manage the child's behavior at home. The children who completed this program demonstrated significant improvements in disruptive behaviors at school with respect to their social skills and academic performance, but they only showed moderate improvements for behavioral problems in the home. It's possible the interventions need further adaptations for older children.

Collaborative Life Skills

Yet another program, called *Collaborative Life Skills*, targets children in elementary school. It also includes BPT, BCM, and child skills training components, but in this program, all of the interventions are implemented in the school by mental health personnel who are known as Learning Support Professionals. The program involves ten weekly BPT and child skills training groups, which are conducted by the Learning Support Professionals at the child's school. Additionally, these mental health personnel conduct a 30 - 60 minute orientation meeting for teachers, and they coordinate two or three meetings between teachers, parents and the child in order to develop a school daily report that will complement a home daily report. Children in this program showed big improvements in behaviors associated with ODD as well as ADHD at home, and they showed moderate improvements at school. They also improved in other areas of their social life as well as with organizational skills and academic tasks.

Summer Treatment Programs

There are also more intensive interventions for children in grades one through eleven. One example is the *Summer Treatment Programs* that use child skills training as well as BPT and a similar BCM intervention in a summer camp setting. Children attend this program for nine hours each day for eight weeks. There, they engage in various activities like sports, art and academic classes while counselors maintain a behavior management system. There are also BPT sessions and medication evaluations and management. These programs have shown moderate to major improvements in symptoms related to both ADHD and ODD/CD. Moreover, they are rated more successful in a variety of domains by the parents, teachers and counselors. It is not clear, however, if the benefits continue after the intensive treatment is finished.

Fast Track

While the previously described interventions have helped reduce symptoms in young people with ODD/CD and/or ADHD, none are specific to the youth at the highest risk of developing more severe conduct problems, that is, those children who show severe conduct problems at a very early age. For these children, this extremely intensive, multi-component program was developed. It contains the same components--BPT, BCM, and child skills training--as the other programs, but is implemented over a longer period of time and was developed to address those environmental mechanisms that both trigger the child and maintain patterns of inappropriate behavior in at-risk children. At-risk children include those who are consistently involved in parent-child conflicts, have suffered from peer rejection, and the like.

Fast Track includes child skills training and BPT components which are implemented in two-hour after school sessions over a 22 week period during the first grade, then bi-weekly in 11 sessions in the second grade, and finally, monthly for 9 months in the third through fifth grades. Additionally, teachers utilize behavioral strategies and help teach skills in emotional understanding, communication, friendship, social problem solving and self-control. When the child enters middle school, there are joint and separate parent and youth groups that tackle adolescent issues like sex education, peer pressure and parental monitoring. Individualized interventions for children in the seventh through tenth grade included a minimum of monthly sessions as well as more intensive, targeted interventions to address particularly resistant problems.

The program showed improvement in aggressive and disruptive behaviors in elementary school, but there was less improvement in the middle school ages. However, the program did significantly reduce the lifetime prevalence of conduct problems in those children who scored at the highest level of risk (highest 3 percent) in their initial assessment. Parents of children with ODD reported almost 20 percent fewer conduct problems in children who had completed the *Fast Track* program, and the benefits continued for at least two years after the program had ended. Results were similar for children with ADHD and CD. These results indicate that, although this is a time- and labor-intensive endeavor, it is effective for those children in the highest risk group for developing conduct problems.

Multimodal Interventions: As with multi-component interventions, multimodal interventions have also shown considerable success in helping manage disruptive behavioral problems. These are the interventions that utilize both medication as well as psychosocial interventions to alleviate behavioral disruptions, and they have been shown to be the optimal intervention for both ADHD and ODD. One of the most important factors when utilizing a multimodal approach is to ensure that the medication dosage is sufficient, and the psychosocial interventions should be designed to address problems related to ODD/CD as well as any comorbidities. There are a couple of different multimodal intervention therapies that provide good examples for discussion.

Multisystemic Therapy

This type of therapy can address several problems simultaneously. It involves coordinating multiple interventions using a team of service providers who work in various contexts to comprehensively address the various disorders. The goal of this therapy is to prevent having to remove a child from the home, either for residential treatment or because of placement in juvenile detention. This program utilizes BPT, BCM, child skills training, and pharmacotherapy. It implements these various interventions within an ecological framework which might include peer groups, the child's school, the immediate and extended family, the child's neighborhood, community groups and other contexts where the child is active.

The therapy involves the availability of medical professionals 24 hours a day, seven days a week as needed. It typically lasts anywhere between three and five months, and it has proven very effective for children with severe ODD, CD, and ADHD as well as children who have problems with substance abuse. The combination of intervention strategies are typically specific to individual needs.

Multidimensional Treatment Foster Care

This type of intervention includes medication as well as psychosocial approaches for children with severe CD. These children are placed in foster homes rather than out-of-home placements like residential treatment centers or juvenile detention. There is some variability between this therapy and the multisystemic intervention described above, but in general, children receive skills and behavioral training from a therapist and behavioral support specialist. They also are in the care of a foster parent trained in BPT, and they engage in family therapy with their biological family. Additionally, they receive psychiatry services as necessary, and there is a program supervisor who coordinates all of these services.

The child receives weekly therapy sessions, both individually and with their family, and they also meet two times per week for anywhere from two to six hours each session with a behavioral support specialist. The length of the therapy is typically between six and nine months, at the end of which, the goal is to reunify the child with their biological family. This type of intervention has been shown to reduce aggressive behavioral problems in both girls and boys, and it also reduces the need for permanent out-of-home placements.

Parent Management Training Programs and Family Therapy:

This type of therapy will instruct parents and family members in the management of the child's behavior. Family members and other caregivers are instructed in positive reinforcement techniques as well as more effective disciplinary actions. Research has shown that this is one of the most effective ways to reduce the inappropriate behavior in children of any age who have symptoms of ODD. This type of therapy focuses on helping parents to respond to their child's behavior in positive ways. They learn disciplinary techniques and age-appropriate supervision that will help diffuse the objectionable behavior. This type of training is so effective that it has become the treatment of choice for many mental health professionals, and it is based on the following principles:

- An increase in positive parenting practices like supportive, consistent supervision and discipline.
- A decrease in negative parenting practices like using harsh punishment and focusing solely on negative behaviors with no positive reinforcement for good behavior.
- Consistent punishment for disruptive types of behavior.
- Predictable, immediate parental responses to inappropriate behavior.

Effective Parent Management Tips

Parent responses to their children's behaviors is a huge part of managing ODD or any other behavioral disorder. There are a number of ways parents can adjust their own behaviors to help the situation and avoid adding to the circumstances that trigger their children. Here are a few tips for how parents can help their children and improve their chances of minimizing the unacceptable behavior:

- **Have open and honest communication**: This is harder than what it seems for most adults. You know that they have done something wrong, and you know what has triggered them, but helping your child realize what they did was wrong can test your patience. You have to talk to your child, but at the same time, hold your tongue. You cannot immediately judge what they have done. If you immediately snap at them when they do something wrong or if they have said something inappropriate in reactive aggression, they will not be opening up to you anymore. You have to act as a legal mediator for your child when they open up to you. Sometimes, you need to speak in a way that addresses yourself in the third person, so the child has an easier visualization of why Mom is not happy when he hurt his brother. You should also do this as lovingly as you can. Having an open relationship back and forth with your child is important and should continue throughout adulthood. You should also respect their privacy and decisions in order to keep that line open. Violating their trust in you by exerting your dominance over them can mean that they will sever this direct line with you, so tread lightly and remember the goal is to help them regulate their own behavior.

- **Connecting events and situations**: When you discover a pattern that triggers your child, do not call them out on it right away. Open that line of communication with them and then present the pattern that you have seen in a non-judgmental way. Do not corner them into thinking that you have been observing their every move as that can also backfire.

Perhaps you can say something like, "Whenever (Situation) happens, you (reaction). It also happened during the time when (situation) when you (reaction). Is that what you usually do? Don't you think it's better to (suggestion)?"

This way, you can still give them a choice to answer yes or no. Then you can let them know why you think it's wrong and what they can do next time so that they won't hurt other people. Again, it's to provide them a plan for the next time which is vital to getting the behavior under control. It's also a useful way to let them know what could trigger that behavior from them.

- **Physical manifestations:** When your child gets triggered by something or someone, oftentimes there are physical manifestations of their behavior. Did their heartbeat rapidly increase? Was their breathing rapid and were their cheeks warm? Were their hands cold and their muscles tensed up? There are many other physical manifestations of stress as well as other types of physical symptoms that show up when there are triggers. Make sure to ask your child if they had felt any of these symptoms and when they noticed it happening. This might be a less confrontational way to approach your child. Knowing that their condition is like an illness, they will approach it in the same way as with an illness and think that a doctor is exactly what they need. You can also teach them that whenever they feel these signs again, to try to act differently since they know what kind of behavior might be coming.
- **Cueing:** Allow yourself and your child to practice with a hand signal that will serve as an alert to them when the trigger is present. This way, they are alerted beforehand and can think about what will happen. If you also practice what needs to be done when your child is triggered, the likelihood of your child's defiant behavior will be less. It is also advisable to add several cues so that there is a repetitiveness in reminders to them.
- **Checking In:** If you noticed that your child did acknowledge the cue but didn't do their part of the bargain, it would be a good idea to pull your child to the side when things have subsided so you can speak to them in private. You want to make sure no one sees. You can calmly discuss with your child what happened and

discuss why he was not able to put into practice what you had rehearsed previously. It may feel unnatural for them at first, but always reassure them that you will always be there to support them. You should remind them, however, of the potential consequences. It's important to do this in a non-threatening way as you don't want to create further distress in your child.
- **Positive Reinforcement**: Parents are often trained in developing skills that utilize positive reinforcement to respond to problems that arise in their child with ODD. The benefits of positive reinforcement include helping your child acquire new skills that will lead to increased independence and higher self-esteem, providing your child with additional motivation that helps them continue to progress, and keeping your child focused on the task at hand. The four most commonly used types of reinforcement include:

1. Social praise and recognition like high 5s, hugging, kissing and clapping.
2. Tangible rewards such as toys.
3. Favorite food rewards like ice cream or chocolate, especially effective for children who don't respond verbally.
4. A token economic reward like an allowance or additional money.

The Benefits of Praise

This is a good place to talk briefly about praising your child. It's important that your children feel they are accepted for who they are, even if they suffer from a disorder like ODD. It's critical that you are consistent in your actions as a parent, and you need to show your child unconditional love, even when they act out. They need that to build their sense of self-confidence and self-worth. Toward this end, it's vital that you recognize and praise your child's positive behaviors. This is true for any child, but particularly for one with ODD. Moreover, your praise should be specific and immediate, for example, "I really like how you helped your sister with that puzzle. That was so nice of you." By being specific, your child knows exactly why they are being praised, and it will not only encourage them to continue behaving in an appropriate manner, it will build their self-esteem.

It's also important that you are a good role model for them. You don't want to engage in power struggles with them or with anyone else. You also want to stick to consistent schedules, because children are more comfortable if they have a routine so that they will know what to expect. Additionally, you can use routines to set boundaries for their behavior and how they spend their time. Part of that time should include interaction with you and the entire family. That helps build critical social skills. In short, you want to establish consistent routines, lavish your child with praise, be firm but fair in your discipline, and make sure everyone in the house gets the same praise and the same consequences for their actions. You should never focus on just one child, particularly the child with ODD. They will pick up on that and see it as an opportunity to control the situation. So, spread the love, and remember, nothing will upend all your good intentions faster than being inconsistent!

Seeing improvement in your child

Helping your child identify their triggers requires constant repetition and practice. As a parent, it may be tiring but knowing that in the end that your child will improve, and hopefully, outgrow their defiant behavior is a great reward in and of itself. Just make sure you keep the lines of communication open and proactively reach out to initiate the conversation between you and your child. It should be a calm, supportive and open dialogue. Having this direct line to their parents reminds the child that they have someone they can vent to without being judged. You will also need to allow your child some room for error when you see new triggers and come up with unique ways to address them. You are looking at years of needing to consistently help your child to eventually not only identify the triggers, but anticipate them and learn techniques to avoid those stressful situations.

Imagine starting this exercise when your child starts kindergarten. You ask them not only about their day but how they felt when a certain stressful situation came up. Even if they were not directly involved in the story they tell you, you will have insight into how they think. You will add entries in your notebook, and over time, you can identify some patterns and help your child with them. For them, this allows them to consistently practice putting into words how they feel. By the time they are in middle school, they become eloquent enough and confident enough to share their secrets because they know you will respect them. Come to think of it, this technique is great for adults in the workplace, too!

The bottom line is they now have the tools needed to manage their emotions and prevent their behavior because they know what triggers them. If they do not upset as many people, then they will likely encounter less aggressive behavior in their life. You can then be more secure and feel better that you did your best helping your child improve. Your ultimate goal is to provide them with the life skills they need to survive and thrive in a world that has little sympathy for aggressive behaviors. By consistently working with your child and adapting treatment methods to match their changing triggers and reactive behaviors, you're giving your child the gift of an independent, normal, happy, healthy life. That's why it's important not to give up, but like Kim, keep looking for new methods that work best for your child and your family.

Chapter Summary

In this chapter, we've discussed various treatment options for helping your child gain more control over their aggressive, negative behaviors. Specifically, we've discussed the following topics:

- Diagnosing ODD.
- Ways to help your mental health provider in establishing a diagnosis.
- The treatment options available for your child.
- Effective parent management tips.
- Seeing improvement in your child's behavior.

In the next chapter, we'll discuss preventative measures to take to keep your child from developing ODD as well as strategies for helping your child live with ODD.

5
PREVENTATIVE MEASURES AND HELPFUL ACTIVITIES FOR CHILDREN WITH ODD

Most experts agree that ODD cannot be prevented, but it can be mitigated by minimizing the defiant behaviors. Typically, this type of training needs to start early, and in fact, many techniques are also good for children who have not been diagnosed with a behavioral problem. Basically, they're just good parenting techniques. Let's take a look at a few strategies parents can implement that may help to minimize any behavioral problems before they get started.

1. **Set up clear expectations ahead of time**. By clearly establishing your expectations before engaging in any activities, your child will know what they need to do to earn privileges for complying with what you want from them. This is more effective than punishing the child when they don't meet your expectations. Children respond well to firm boundaries and clear goals. While you, as a parent, need to establish those goals, it's also helpful to let your child have a say in the privileges they will receive if they do what's expected of them. That gives them a sense of pride and motivates them to do what they need to do.

If your child gets distracted as they are working toward a goal, remind them of what they will receive if they get back on track rather than threatening some kind of punishment if they don't. This gives your child a sense of empowerment, because they have it within their own hands to earn the privilege they helped choose. It's also a good lesson in self-motivation.

2. Use transition warnings. Transition warnings are when you give your child notice that they are going to need to stop doing what they are doing and transition to another activity, and you do this before they actually have to refocus their attention. For example, "In 10 minutes, you'll need to turn off the TV and come eat dinner," or, "When this show is over, you need to come do your homework." You should also follow these transition warnings with reminders as the time gets closer, for example, "In two minutes, you'll need to turn the TV off." For children who don't yet have a concept of time, you can use a visual reminder like a timer, for example, "When the bell goes off you have three minutes," or, "When the clock sounds five times, it's time to come eat your dinner."

3. Use empathetic statements. You want your child to understand that you know how he or she feels, particularly when you are asking them to do something. You can probably understand how you would feel if someone came barging into your room and ordered you to do something. Your child feels the same way, and if you can show them, for example, you understand that they might not feel like going to bed, but they need to get rest for school in the morning, that's a much more empathetic way to get them to comply. It's also a good idea to reassure them that they will have more time to do the things they love to do. That will help them feel more comfortable with complying with your request.

4. Use positive directives and don't use the word "can." When asking your child to do something, you should always use a confident, calm tone of voice. Rather than saying, "Can you turn off the TV and come eat dinner," say, "Turn off the TV and come eat dinner." It's even better if, instead of telling your child what not to do, you tell them what to do. You might try redirecting them by giving them an alternate activity like, "Let's put this puzzle together," or, "Let's go to the playground." Finally, it's best to give them an explanation as to why you're asking them to do what you want them to do. For example, "Stop jumping on the couch because you might fall and you can also damage the couch." That way they understand why you're asking them to change what they're doing.

5. Acknowledge healthy behaviors. When your child opts to engage in healthy activities like eating an apple instead of candy, or when they respond to a frustration using appropriate behaviors, be sure to acknowledge those good choices. As discussed earlier, be specific in your praise. If you notice they are being particularly diligent with their homework, you could say, "You are really focused on your homework. Good job. I'm very proud of you." If they opt to use an appropriate behavior in response to what you know typically triggers them, say something like, "I'm really impressed with how you handled that situation." Such positive reinforcement serves to remind your child which behaviors you like to see, and it boosts their self-esteem and confidence.

6. Pick your battles carefully. Your young child might be playing in the dirt, and maybe you find it unpleasant, but if he or she is not in danger of being hurt or hurting or disrespecting someone else, give them a little freedom. Remember, they are exploring their world, and you want to boost their confidence in doing so. Let them explore as much as is safe and practical to do, and save the battle for something more important.

7. Give them as much freedom as possible. Wherever you can give them freedom and control over their own choices, do so. For example, let them choose which color shirt they want to wear or which homework to focus on first. That helps them make good choices, and it gives them a sense of control over their life.

8. Say what you mean, and mean what you say. We've mentioned the importance of following through on consequences if your child becomes defiant, but it's a great general rule to help prevent unruly, defiant behaviors as well. If your child knows from the get-go that you don't make empty threats, they will be less inclined to defy your wishes. Likewise, if they learn that you won't really do what you said you would, they will continue to push the limits.

9. Make a schedule. Wherever you can, create a schedule for your child. This should include their chores, homework, self-care tasks like bathing and brushing teeth and any fun activities. You should include your child in the process of creating the schedule so they will feel a sense of ownership in planning their time. It will also teach them how to best manage their time, which will alleviate certain stressors. You should arrange the schedule so that fun activities are interspersed with chores and other non-preferred activities. Structuring your child's time can help alleviate impulsive behaviors. You'll want to set the schedule up in such a way that the child can complete one part before moving on to the next part.

10. Don't argue, negotiate, lecture, or respond sarcastically to your child. As the parent, you need to always remain calm, confident and in control. By resisting the temptation to resort to arguing with your child or negotiating the rules you've set, you let them know the boundaries for their behavior. As mentioned, show empathy when you talk to your child about the rules and what you want them to do, but if they start to argue or throw a tantrum, simply let them know that you've told them the rules and you're not going to talk about it anymore. If you give attention to their tantrums, they'll use that tactic again in the future. Instead, ignore it and once they have calmed down, praise them for calming themselves down, and then be prepared to listen if they want to talk with you about their feelings. After listening to them and validating their feelings, direct them back to the task you expected them to do.

Of course, you should protect your child from harm if they are trying to hurt themselves or others, but don't negotiate or give into temper tantrums. If you are genuinely concerned for your child's safety, or for anyone else's, contact a crisis center.

THERE IS NO SINGLE METHOD THAT WILL WORK FOR EVERY CHILD, BUT these techniques are backed up by research as well as countless personal experiences. They work well most of the time, regardless of whether your child has ODD or not. By providing your child with a nurturing home environment where their feelings are validated, set loving but firm boundaries, and include fair, immediate disciplinary measures as well as immediate and specific praise for appropriate behavior, you can minimize defiant behavior even in children genetically predisposed to ODD.

You cannot completely protect your child, but you can control the environment in which they live. You can provide unconditional love and quality time together. With consistent, caring parenting, you can teach your child to respect authority. In fact, there are some experts who believe that ODD develops following a sequence of experiences that begins with ineffective parenting practices that leads to defiance of other authority figures and poor peer relationships. As these experiences are compounded one after the other, ODD develops as a consistent pattern of behavior. Early detection of the condition along with improving communication skills, conflict resolution skills, parenting skills and anger management skills can help to disrupt that negative pattern and decrease the defiant behaviors. The goal of early intervention is to help get the child back on a normal growth and development trajectory so they will experience an improvement in their quality of life. Here are a few other tips that can help you create a loving, nurturing, and firm but fair environment:

- Always show your child unconditional love and acceptance.
- Both parents should spend quality time with your child, if possible.
- Demonstrate interest in your child's life and their daily activities.
- Parents shouldn't fight in front of the children.
- Give your child unconditional support as they express their dreams.
- Seek treatment for any problems early in the process.

SELF-REGULATION ACTIVITIES

Another important factor in children with disruptive behaviors is the problem they have with self-regulation. This refers to their ability to maintain appropriate interest for any specific situation as well as their ability to generate both appropriate behavioral and sensory responses for the environmental stimuli present. It also refers to their ability to control themselves; that is, to monitor and control their own behavior, their attention, their motor output, their emotions and their social interactions.

Self-regulation is exemplified by a child who is able to maintain his composure, problem-solve, or ask for help in a given situation, for example when another child takes his toy or understanding to keep his voice quiet in a library. In school, this means understanding that he has to attend class and stay at his desk while the teacher is talking, or stay with his class as he exits for a fire drill, or even something as simple as walking in line in the hallway. Being able to self-regulate involves complex cognition and sensory systems, and many children struggle with one or more areas, making self-regulation challenging for them. There are, however, activities that can help children develop skills in this area, which can then minimize disruptive behavioral problems associated with ODD.

Helping Children Self-Regulate

Research has shown that there are some games and fun activities you can use to effectively promote your child's ability to self-regulate. The kinds of games and therapy tools that help are those that prompt your child to plan and problem-solve as well as pay attention, remember things, and practice motor control. There are also some exercises that help your child practice calming themselves, increase self-awareness, and promote mindfulness. The following are examples of these types of activities:

- **Red Light, Green Light:** You probably remember this game from your own childhood. One child stands a distance away from the other players. This child is "it." The child who is "it" turns their back on the other children and yells, "Green light!" The other children move towards "it." Then, the child who is "it" spins around and yells, "Red light!" Any child still moving when they yell red light must go back to the starting line. When a child reaches "it," they tag him or her. They become the new "it," and the game starts again. This game teaches your child to be able to follow instructions and play with others.
- **Simon Says:** Another childhood classic that teaches children to listen closely to instructions. The rules are that one child is Simon and tells the other children, "Simon says...," followed by a command like, "Raise your right arm." The other children should only do the action if Simon says to do it. If the child just says, for example, "Raise your arm," with no, "Simon says," in front of it, then they should not follow the instruction. If the child does not start the command with Simon says and the other

children do the action anyway, they are out. Again, this kind of game teaches children to listen carefully and follow instructions.

- **Partner Obstacle Course:** This game teaches your child teamwork and social skills. Your child and a friend have to hold hands while they navigate an obstacle course you set up. You might, for example, have them jump over a pillow while holding hands or go up and down a step. They must work with their partner to successfully get through the obstacle course.
- **Duck Duck Goose:** One child is "it," and the rest of the children sit in a circle. "It" walks around the circle tapping children on the head and saying, "Duck." When "it" taps someone on the head and says, "Goose," that child gets up and runs after "it" trying to catch him or her. If he does catch him, he gets to sit back down, but if "it" gets around the circle and sits in the place left by that child, then that child becomes the new "it." Again, your child learns to listen carefully, react appropriately, and interact with others.
- **Freeze Tag:** With this game, children sit perfectly still until their friends tag them to "unfreeze" them. It's a great game for self-regulation and self-control as well as working on social skills.
- **Partner Painting:** This is a great activity to help teach kids to cooperate with each other, and it also helps them improve their visual motor and fine motor skills. You simply set two pieces of paper for painting or drawing next to one another. Designate one partner as the leader and instruct him to paint a picture. You might say, for example, paint a picture of a house. The other child is instructed to copy what he or she sees the first child drawing. They are not told what the first child is drawing. They work together to produce the two pictures.
- **Hide and Seek:** Another childhood classic where one

child counts to 20 or more while other children hide. When the child is done counting, he goes to find the hidden children. Can they stay hidden and quiet while their friend tries to find them? That's what helps teach them self-regulation.

- **Wacky Relay**: This game teaches children to work together as they carry an object together for a specified distance. They carry the object by pressing it between them. You might, for example, have them carry a ball by pressing it between each other using their backs or elbows, shoulders, chins, foreheads, or other body parts. They definitely have to work together to get the job done.
- **Freeze Dance**: This game helps children regulate their movements and behavior. While the music is playing, they dance, but when it stops, they freeze in place. If they don't do that, they are out.
- **Musical Chairs**: This is another classic that helps children regulate their behavior, both within the game and when they're out. You set a number of chairs in a circle. There should be one less chair than there are children. While the music plays, the children walk around in a circle outside the chairs. When the music stops, they must sit in a chair. One child will not be able to sit because there aren't enough chairs. If a child can't sit, they are out.
- **Mirror, Mirror**: In this game, you pair your child with another child and designate one as the leader. The leader then makes movements, and the other child must 'mirror' those movements. This helps kids develop coordination as well as social skills.
- **Counting Down**: This is a great anticipation activity that helps children learn to wait, and to control themselves while waiting. To do this, set out a beanbag chair and have the child countdown--3...2...1...Jump!--before jumping into the bean bag chair. You could also have children count

down to starting a race or some other activity. By having to wait to begin, they learn self-control.
- **Hand Clapping Games:** These are also classics. You might remember, "Patty cake, patty cake, baker's man, bake me a cake as fast as you can!" This is recited while clapping hands in specific patterns. It teaches children coordination, helps them with memory and cognitive skills, and emphasizes cooperative play.
- **Hedbanz:** This is another fun game where children must work together and control themselves. In a headband, the children place a card with a picture on it. The child wearing the headband can't see the card, so they don't know what's on it. They have to ask questions of the other children who can see the card. Those children need to answer the questions without telling the child what the picture is since the child has to figure it out for themselves. This game teaches children to interact with each other, practice self-control, and build cognitive skills.
- **Dancing:** There are few things that children love as much as dancing. They can practice different dance styles including ones that involve dancing with a partner. This helps build coordination as well as cooperation.
- **Suspend:** This is a game that requires patience, cognitive skills and coordination. Children must balance pieces of the game one on top of the other. They have to carefully consider where and how to balance the pieces so the whole structure doesn't fall. Additionally, to be successful, children must regulate the force of their movements.
- **Jenga:** This game is similar to Suspend in that children must carefully remove pieces of the tower without having the whole thing come tumbling down. It requires careful movements and cognitive as well as cooperative skills.
- **Balloon Volleyball:** This is volleyball that can be played indoors, because it is played with a balloon. Children have to learn to control their movements given the more

unpredictable nature of the balloon, and they also have to learn to cooperate with their teammates.
- **Operation:** This is another classic that requires careful movements. It helps children develop coordination, and they also learn to play well with other children.
- **Simon:** This is a game that helps build memory skills. Lights of different colors light up on the board in different sequences. The challenge is for the child to remember and repeat the light sequence. It can be played alone or with other players. In the case of multiple players, your child learns social skills.
- **Sequenced Motor Tasks:** This requires no equipment. You simply have your child do a sequence of motor tasks. For example, you might ask them to jump three times, then hop twice, and then, stand on one food while they count to five. It requires coordination as well as memory skills, and it can be done with just one child or several.
- **Bop It:** This game has different commands that players have to respond to correctly and quickly to stay in the game. They might be asked, for example, to "drink it," or, "hammer it," and they have to respond with the correct movements or else they're out of the game. Children must respond correctly and quickly which helps build both coordination and cognitive skills. They also learn to respond appropriately when other children make a mistake.
- **Spot It:** This is a great game for building visual and social skills. Children must spot the one symbol that two cards have in common. They need a quick eye to find the symbol, and they need to cope with losing when they don't spot it.

Mindfulness Activities

Mindfulness activities are another great way to help children learn to self-regulate. Several of these techniques also serve to help children calm down and survey their feelings. There are a number of techniques that are helpful for children at risk for behavioral problems like ODD. Let's take a look at several that can be easily used to help children stay mindful of their bodies, thoughts, and emotions.

1. Breathing Techniques: There are several breathing techniques that can help children regulate their breath and calm themselves down. It's often helpful to have children, particularly young children, engage in movement while focusing on their breath. For example, you might have them trace an infinity symbol while breathing in and out. That can help them achieve a smooth, even, breath cycle. Another helpful visualization technique is to have them visualize that they are filling up a balloon as they inhale air into their bellies.

Another great breathing exercise for children is alternate nostril breathing. They breath in through one nostril--for example, their right nostril--and then, out through the left. Then, they can change the sides. This keeps them focused on their breathing. Counting while they inhale, holding their breath for a specified count, and then exhaling to a specified count is another technique that helps them focus and control their breath. You can also have them simply count their breaths--1 on the inhale, 2 on the exhale, 3 on the inhale, and so on until they reach 10. Then, they can start over at 1 again.

It can also help to utilize visualization techniques along with controlled breathing. A great one is to have children visualize they are standing on the beach as they're breathing. With each inhale, they are drawing a wave up onto the sand, and on each exhale the water recedes again. You can also place something on the child's belly so they will actually have something to move as they breathe in and out. Additionally, as with tracing the infinity symbol, you can also have kids trace another symbol, like a square, with their finger as they breathe. Finally, having kids engage in slow, thoughtful movement as they breathe is another excellent way to get them focused and keep them interested. You might have them walk slowly in a particular pattern, for example.

2. Guided Meditation for Kids: Guided meditation is a great way to practice self-regulation and help kids get in touch with their bodies, thoughts, and emotions. The challenge often comes with helping them remain still and focus on their sensations. This is particularly true for younger children. It's important to consider a few things as you prepare to help your kids meditate.

First of all, your child needs to be in a comfortable, safe place where they can relax. That will help you get them in the right mindset to get the most benefit out of the experience. Here are few things to consider to help them feel comfortable:

- **Seated or lying down:** If you're planning a longer meditation, it might be better to have them lay down, but you could always begin with a seated meditation and then transition to a full resting pose.
- **Lights and sound:** You'll want to dim the lights as you read a meditation script, and you can also choose some calming music to create the right vibe. You should reduce or eliminate any distracting noises as well, and if all else fails, silence is always a good choice.
- **Length of the meditation:** To choose the length of the script, you have to consider your child's individual attention span. If you're just starting out, it's best to begin with a shorter script until you know what your child is able to tolerate. Additionally, you don't want to incorporate too much information in your script. Be sure that you give your child enough time to integrate what they're hearing.
- **Tone and pace:** Be mindful of your tone as you read the script. You want to project a calm confidence so your child

can feel relaxed and safe. You should read the script slowly, but make sure you read it quickly enough to keep them engaged.
- **Flexibility**: Be sure that you maintain a flexible attitude. Things might not go as you had planned it. Your child might be more restless than usual, and it's always possible difficult emotions might surface. As with adults, the responses a child has to meditative activities can be unpredictable. Be sure to ground yourself in compassion before beginning and be open to whatever might arise.

With these tips in mind, the following is a script that is a good one for younger children involving colors:

- Let's focus on the present moment. Can you feel your toes? What position are they in? Can you feel your shoes on your feet? How about your legs? Can you feel your knees? Are they warm or cold? Are they sitting on something hard or soft? How about your tummy, can you feel it? What does your belly button feel like? What about your neck, can you feel your neck? Can you feel air on your neck? How about your forehead? Can you feel it? (Allow your child to think about or answer these questions)
- Now, I want you to think about a color you like. What color did you choose? Is it a bright color or a darker color? Is it your favorite color? (Allow for thoughts or answers.)
- Can you look around and find one thing that is the color you've picked? What is it? How big is it? What is its shape? (Allow time for finding an object and answers.)
- Can you find something else that is this color? (Allow enough time to find another object.)
- Let's answer the same questions as the other object. What is it? How big is it? What is its shape like? (Allow for answers.)

- How does this color make you feel? Does it make you feel happy? Does it make you feel sad? Why?
- Okay, now I want you to close your eyes for a moment. Just rest your eyes and take a few deep breaths. Now, we'll count down from five and then you can open your eyes. Ready? Five...four...three...two...one, deep breath, now open your eyes.

3. Zones of Regulation: This is a great way to help children build skills for consciously regulating their own actions, and that then leads to more control and better problem-solving abilities. The idea is to help children understand when they are in different states, which are called zones. Each zone is marked by a different color. In each zone, students will use different strategies or tools to either stay in that zone or move to another zone. These strategies and tools include things like reading the facial expressions of other children, recognizing emotions and gauging one another's mood with a mood meter. The idea is to help students self-regulate as well as to help you identify triggers that lead to less-regulated states.

4. Calming Sensory Activities: These activities involve various strategies for helping children learn to calm themselves down. There are several tips that can help with these activities:

- **Utilizing a quiet place:** Designate a quiet space for your child where they can reduce their exposure to various types of stimuli. This should be a place where your child knows they can go to regroup and calm themselves; they won't be judged or punished for utilizing their quiet space. Additionally, children should have a clear way to indicate they need to use the quiet place, perhaps a visual signal or some other indicator that they need some time alone.
- **Calming tactile activities:** There are a number of ways to help your child calm down using their tactile system. A really simple tool is to make a tactile bin. This can be a

shoebox-sized plastic container, for example, that you can then fill with something like sand, dry rice or dry beans. When your child needs to calm themselves, they can simply run their hands through the material in the bin. Another method you can use for kids who feel completely overwhelmed is to hug them with a weight blanket or a weighted stuffed animal or even a beanbag chair. This provides a full-body tactile method for helping them calm down.

- **Calming oral input:** This is another helpful method to help kids calm themselves down. Chewing can provide a calming sensation. For this, you can use gum or other chewy snacks; there are online stores that sell safe products for kids who like to chew as a means to calm down. These items include things they can wear which are safe to chew on like pendants or bracelets. If you don't have something like that, it's also effective to have children suck against resistance as happens if they are trying to suck a thick smoothie through a straw. It can also work to have them blow something around. You might, for example, have them blow a feather across a table. These are all oral stimulation techniques that can help them calm down.
- **Calming sounds and silence:** Some kids just need a little quiet time to calm things down. You might have your child indicate when they need a little silence visually, and then, if you have to address them, be sure to use a soft, quiet voice when doing so. For these kids, noise reduction headphones might be a great idea to help them block out sounds that make them feel overstimulated. Other kids might benefit from white noise or sounds of nature like a light rain or ocean waves gently lapping at the shore. Even a fan can be a source of calming noise. Calming music is another option.
- **Calming visuals:** Some children are more visually

oriented, and they want less light or natural light to help them calm down. For these children, it will be important to also help them find ways to reduce visual distractions, particularly in learning environments. They may need clutter-free workspaces and limited decorations. To help them calm down, repetitive visual input such as what they see when watching a fish in a fish tank or even watching a bottle filled with water and oil can be very effective. Add a little glitter to that bottle filled with water and oil, and you have a great sensory bottle. For these children, it can also help to have a visual picture schedule so they will know what's coming throughout the day.

- **Calming proprioceptive input:** Some children benefit more from using their bodies in an active way. Proprioceptive work in this sense involves activities like squeezing PlayDoh or a stress ball. It can even be something like pulling against a resistance band, pushing or moving chairs or desks, carrying books, holding a heavy door open or climbing stairs.
- **Calming movements:** These are movements that are repetitive and rhythmic in nature like rocking, gentle swinging or swaying. It's a great way to help your child calm down when they are overstimulated or just feeling overwhelmed. You might want to add a rocking chair to your activity room. An exercise ball is also a good addition that kids can use for these kinds of movements. You can have children engage in row, row, row your boat activities like holding hands with a partner and swaying back and forth or standing while swaying.
- **Yoga:** Yoga is a great way for kids to move their bodies while staying mindful and engaging in an activity that can help to calm them down. It stimulates their proprioceptive system as well as their tactile system and their balance or vestibular system. When combined with breathing

techniques that are synced with the movements, this is a great way for them to calm their entire nervous system.
- **Repetitive, quiet, familiar fine motor and visual tasks:** These kinds of tasks can have a very calming effect for many kids. These are particularly helpful for kids who become overwhelmed easily. These kinds of tasks include things like stringing beads, sorting objects, or counting objects. These can be a great way to start the day in a calm way.
- **Combinations of activities:** Don't be afraid to mix and match these activities to find what's best for your kids. You might, for example, have your child play in a tactile bin while also listening to white noise or quiet music. You could also try something like having them lay in a weighted blanket while watching a sensory bottle or chew gum while sorting differently shaped blocks. Calm breathing techniques can easily be paired with rhythmic rocking or swaying. There are a number of different combinations you can use, so don't be afraid to experiment until you find the right one for your child.

All of these activities are designed to help your child learn how to regulate their own behavior and body. When used in combination with the parenting techniques mentioned earlier, these activities can help your child learn how to control themselves even when they are triggered. This is one of the best ways to prevent disruptive behavior. By helping your child learn different methods to moderate their behavior, you'll be setting them up for success in social situations. They'll also be better able to focus on their studies in school.

CHAPTER SUMMARY

In this chapter, we've reviewed a number of techniques that can help your child learn to recognize and moderate their own behavior. Specifically, we've covered the following topics:

- Strategies parents can use to give their children appropriate boundaries and guidelines for proper behavior.
- Fun activities for children that help them learn how to self-regulate.
- Mindfulness activities that help children calm themselves as necessary.

In the next chapter you will learn about teaching strategies for children with ODD.

6

TEACHING STRATEGIES FOR CHILDREN WITH ODD

When your child is having problems controlling his behavior, it's not enough that you take measures at home to help him understand what is appropriate and how he can control his own behavior. It's important that the child's teachers also participate in behavior management techniques. This is particularly vital given the role that school plays in the socialization process. For your child to learn and practice appropriate social skills, teachers must understand the problem and how to manage disruptive behavior when it occurs in the classroom setting.

One thing that has been shown to help is a daily report card where the child is 'graded' each day on his performance in specific domains of behavior where there is a demonstrated need for improvement. The child is then rewarded when he meets daily goals for improvement. This alone, however, is not enough. There are a number of other methods teachers can employ in the classroom to help those children with ODD. Let's take a look at several options for the classroom.

TEACHER STRATEGIES

While there is no single, magic strategy that will work across the board, there are some techniques that have been shown to be effective. These include the following:

- **Ensure the student receives positive teacher recognition.** This can mean something as simple as greeting the student daily when they arrive in the classroom or stopping by their desk to ask them how they are doing. This can help turn around those teacher-student relationships that are already strained.
- **Proactive intervention for off-task students can prevent escalation.** Teachers need to be particularly vigilant in the classroom when students with disruptive behavioral problems are present. This is so they can intervene when they witness mild misbehaviors to prevent an escalation of the problem into something more serious. It sounds simple, but it requires that teachers make a concerted effort to stay vigilant.
- **Speak calmly and respectfully in all interactions with students.** This is a good rule for any student, but it is critical for students with ODD. Sarcastic responses or raising your voice can easily set a student with behavioral problems off. Then, it's difficult to get them calmed down. This is not to say that a teacher should tolerate misbehavior, but there are strategies to de-escalate the situation before it becomes more serious.

In interactions with any student, the teacher should strive to stay emotionally neutral and professional at all times, but this is particularly true when dealing with a defiant student. Negative reprimands, raising your voice, or responding with sarcasm will further trigger defiant behavior. Thus, when responding to such students, stay calm and keep your voice neutral. It's also a good idea to keep it brief since longer responses give the defiant student more control over the situation. Additionally, some students can come to see any attention, even negative attention, as a reward for their behavior. By keeping your responses short and to the point, you can help prevent that from happening.

- **Be firm, but don't judge.** When intervening with a misbehaving student, teachers need to let the student know that they are unconditionally valued and accepted, but that misbehavior will not be tolerated. It's important to reassure the student that they, as an individual, are not a problem; it's their behavior that cannot be allowed in the classroom setting.
- **Keep the goal in mind.** The ultimate goal of any discipline with a student who has ODD is to teach them more positive ways of interacting and behaving in the classroom environment. Whenever possible, positive reinforcement is a better option to punishment, which doesn't tend to improve student behaviors in the long run and can negatively affect school performance and motivation.
- **Develop a crisis response plan.** When there are students who struggle with disruptive behavioral disorders like ODD in the classroom, it's vital to have a plan that can be implemented in the event that one or more students are triggered into aggressive behaviors that threaten their own safety or the safety of others. It's critical that teachers, parents and school administrators all understand the plan, and that everyone who plays a role in the plan knows what they are supposed to do. You can never predict or necessarily prepare for every possibility, but you are more likely to get a good outcome by staying calm, acting consistently and fairly, and following pre-planned strategies when students are misbehaving.

Toward this end, it's important for teachers to have a predetermined set of consequences for misbehavior in the classroom. Some misbehaviors should be handled easily in the classroom while others may need the intervention of school administrators and parents. To begin, list the behaviors that can typically be handled in the classroom. These would be mild misbehaviors. Medium misbehaviors would be those that could result in the student being sent to the principal's office, and serious misbehaviors would require something more such as a phone call to the parents.

Once you have your list of behaviors, write the consequence next to the misbehavior. Of course, the consequences you reserve for the classroom should be minor problems, and if a student displays any behaviors that seriously disrupt the classroom environment or pose a risk to their own safety or that of others, teachers should immediately contact an administrator. By having a predetermined list, however, you can be prepared to set appropriate boundaries in the classroom. You can indicate what is expected of students and the consequences for not behaving appropriately.

Classroom Strategies

While teachers can benefit from acting as described above, there are also some specific classroom strategies that can help to prevent the need for an intervention, and there are some specific disciplinary strategies that can help students better understand how their misbehavior affects others as well as how they plan to improve their behavior going forward. These techniques integrate the student into the process of correcting their own behavior rather than simply having authority figures impose corrections on them. The following strategies can help:

1. **Cool-Down Breaks**: Teachers can designate an area of the classroom, or an area outside the classroom, where a student can take a break if they feel particularly triggered. This is an option that should be available to all students in the classroom so that no one is singled out. Before sending them on a cool-down break,

however, teachers should make it clear that once the student has calmed down, they must be willing to talk about the situation with them so they can process their feelings. Try something like, "John, I really want to talk with you about why you're feeling so upset right now, but it's important that you calm down before we do that. So, please take five minutes to cool down, and when you're feeling calm, come to my desk so we can talk about it."

2. **Open-Ended Questions:** As teachers investigate what triggered a child's defiant response, it's helpful to use open-ended questions. These include neutral questions, the goal of which is to gather more information before deciding how to respond. These are the 'who,' 'what,' 'where,' 'when,' and 'how' questions that will help them more clearly understand the problem and develop possible solutions. Sample questions include, "What do you think made you so angry as you were speaking with John?" and, "Where were you when you first found out you had lost your math book?" These can help you pinpoint the exact trigger for the defiant behavior. One thing to watch out for, however, is that you don't want to ask 'why' questions like, "Why did you fight with Amy?" Those can seem like you're blaming the student, so it's best to avoid asking why and stick to the other facts.

3. **Reflective "Processing" Essay:** When students get into conflicts, a good response is to require that the student write a brief essay detailing their role in the conflict, the role of other participants, what exactly triggered them to respond in the way they did, their suggestions for resolving the current problem, and finally, their suggestions for how to prevent future misbehavior in similar circumstances. Teachers may even want to develop a pre-printed questionnaire that prompts the student to provide this information. Once again, this gives the

student a role in both understanding and mitigating their own aggressive behaviors.

4. **Don't Argue:** Teachers need to avoid becoming entangled in arguments with students. This is true for any student, but it is particularly critical for students with ODD. By arguing or discussing your orders or responses to defiant behavior, you undermine your own authority. You want to always keep your voice in a neutral, professional tone as you simply state that you won't discuss your decisions with the student. You can indicate that you are happy to discuss the student's feelings about your response with them, but they will need to comply with what you have told them to do. This is where it is best to be following a predetermined (and approved by all involved) plan for imposing consequences for misbehavior. If a teacher feels they are being drawn into an argument, they should implement strategies to disengage themselves from the situation. These include things like moving away from the student, and repeating your request in a neutral, but firm, tone of voice.

5. **State the Positive:** It's helpful to modify instructor requests in a way that doesn't trigger a defiant response. If you can put a positive spin on the request, the student is more likely to comply and less likely to feel the need to resist. For example, rather than saying, "I won't help you until you return to your seat," try something like, "I'll be right over to help you with your assignment as soon as you get back to your seat." That phrases your request for the student to return to their seat in a positive light.

6. **Active Listening:** Active listening is carefully listening to what the other person is saying as if it is true, then restating what you heard to confirm you understand the situation well, and then responding with compassion. For a defiant student, this is a vital skill. Students with ODD can become triggered just by the need to voice a

complaint. By using active listening skills, a teacher can demonstrate they respect and care about what the student is experiencing. It also helps the student feel both heard and understood. Use phrases like, "Let me be sure I understand what you're telling me about...," "It sounds to me like you're concerned about...," or "Are you saying..." In each case, you should sum up what you heard the student say, and give them an opportunity to correct any misunderstanding. Then, once you've heard them correctly, it's important to validate their feelings about the situation. From there, you can formulate a strategy to deal with the problem.

7. **Specific Praise, but Don't Embarrass Your Student**: We've talked before about how it's important for kids with ODD to hear specific praise for their actions. In the classroom, it's more of a delicate situation. You want to praise the student, and children with ODD respond well to specific praise, but you don't want to embarrass them. Keep it low-key even though you make it both specific and immediate. For example, you might say something like, "I really want to compliment you on your essay. I was impressed with how well you explored the topic. You did a very good job." If the student is particularly sensitive to public praise, you might just write a note on their graded assignment or arrange to have a private conversation with them. It might even be worth calling the parents to offer your praise.

8. **Positive Attention and Positive Quality**: As mentioned above, it's important for students with ODD to receive positive attention from the teacher, and in fact, they should be positively interacting with the teacher three times as much as they are being reprimanded. This positive attention really cements the relationship between the student and the teacher. But, it's not the only positive quality in the classroom. Moreover, the classroom

environment should be one that is attractive and reinforcing. By structuring lessons around topics of interest to the students, increasing cooperative learning opportunities, and setting the students up to succeed on assignments, the teacher can create a positive environment that students consider a learning refuge as opposed to some kind of punishment.

9. **Student Input:** It's also important to have students with behavioral problems participate in their own behavioral management plan. That gives them a sense of ownership in their own behavior, and that will increase compliance with any plan that is implemented. This is also helpful since they usually know better than anyone what triggers them as well as what calms them down.

10. **Saving Face:** Sometimes students blunder their way into conflicts with teachers, and in order to avoid a full-blown meltdown, it can help to offer the student a way to save face while backing down on their defiance. This tactic is a good one in almost any human interaction. It's easy to let pride get in the way of good sense, but with a face-saving out, everyone can feel like they have been heard. There are several ways to do this. One would be to ask the misbehaving student something like, "What can we do to work together on a solution so that you can remain in class and be successful?" That allows the student to save their dignity while also actively participating in creating a solution. It also shows the student that negotiation is a positive way to resolve a conflict as opposed to defiance, and it helps them avoid more serious consequences.

It can frequently happen that students will initially reply with a sarcastic comment like, "You can stop making me do classwork," and you should ignore those kinds of comments and ask again if there is a reasonable way to work together. Usually, when they are asked a second time, the student will come up with a workable idea to help resolve the situation. If, however, they don't, the teacher should employ the predetermined consequence for the level of misbehavior in that situation.

1. **Proactively De-escalate and Project Calm:** When teachers see that a child is escalating in defiant behaviors, they can help to de-escalate the situation by interrupting the student's anger, and the earlier in the escalation cycle, the better their chances for success. If the defiant behavior is low-level, it might work to try engaging the student in a high-interest activity. This could be something like a computer game or having them assist as the classroom helper. You might also need to remove the student from the classroom to calm the situation down. To do that without it being a punishment, you might ask the student to run an errand to the main office.

Whenever you're engaging with a student whose behavior is escalating, you should project a calm attitude without any anger. Some tips for doing this include things like moving toward the student slowly rather than quickly, don't approach them too closely, speak to them privately in a calm, respectful voice. Avoid using body language that can betray your emotions like staring at the student, placing your hands on your hips, or finger pointing. Remember to keep your comments brief, and if the student's behavior continues to escalate, implement the predetermined higher level consequences.

It's also helpful if you can engage in a brief, relaxation technique prior to responding to a student exhibiting defiant behavior. One example might be to take three deep breaths before responding or mentally counting to 10. This will give you a moment to think about what is an appropriate response, too, so that you're not just reacting to the student's behavior.

2. **Positive Reinforcement:** Teachers should use positive reinforcement techniques wherever possible to encourage appropriate behaviors as the norm for classroom interactions. This involves providing positive attention and incentives for appropriate social and academic behaviors. These are withheld when students

are misbehaving. That helps to shape the student's positive behavior over the long-term.

3. Interaction Approaches: When you do need to interact with a defiant student, whether the misbehaviour escalates or not is often determined by how you structure your verbal requests, how you use "soft" reprimands, and your non-verbal cues. For students with ODD, part of their defiance relates to their sense of freedom to choose. So, teachers can frame their requests to reflect their acknowledgement that, in fact, the student is free to choose. To do this, teachers want to pose their request as a two-part choice, "Either you can...., or you can....." For example, "Susan, you can stay after school to finish your work or you can finish your work in class and you won't need to stay after school. It's your choice." When doing this, you always want to state the negative option first with its consequences, and then state the positive choice.

Another option when you see a student just beginning to misbehave is to use a "soft" reprimand to get them back on track. A soft reprimand can be as simple as a significant look or a quiet word. This simple act can help derail inappropriate behavior before it really gets started. If the soft reprimand doesn't work, you can often pull the student aside for a private conversation or use those predetermined consequences.

Regardless of the nature of the interaction, your body language is important in conveying your message. You want to make sure you're using non-threatening body language as well as a soft tone of voice and strategic pauses while you're talking to help reduce the tension. If a student is agitated, sit next to them rather than standing over them so you're less threatening. Use micro-pauses to indicate your calm attitude, and speak slowly to project a calm, confident attitude. These help prevent further escalation of the situation.

4. Validate Emotions: The best way to validate a student's emotions is to acknowledge them. If you observe that a student seems angry, by labeling the emotion that appears to be causing the behavior, you can help the student to talk about it and figure out what triggered it. Now, no one can ever know with certainty what feelings someone else is experiencing, and so, you want to be careful to state that the student appears or seems to be or sounds angry, upset, sad or whatever emotional label is appropriate. In other words, don't assume that is the correct emotion.

Ask the student something like, "Karen, you seem angry. Can you tell me what's wrong?" Another example is, "Steve, you sound like you're frustrated. Can you tell me what's up?" This helps the student identify the emotion they're feeling, and by labeling it, they will often then feel inclined to open up to you and talk about what caused them to feel that way. This helps them to use a direct form of communication to talk about their feelings rather than the indirect way of acting out with inappropriate behaviors. That will help them process their feelings so they can let them go and move on.

5. Call a Buddy for Help: If all else fails and the teacher feels their frustration level rising to the point where they are having trouble controlling their own emotions, it can help to send the student to a neighboring classroom so that both the teacher and the student can take a break. Of course, this should only be used in the case of mildly non-compliant students, but having a teaching 'buddy' who agrees to take the student when you need a brief respite from their antics can help everyone calm down. Clearly, these timeouts should be something that are only infrequently used, and they should be discontinued altogether if the student sees them as a reward or a way to avoid doing their classwork. But, in the right amount, these can be a helpful way to reset interactions with some students.

A Deeper Understanding

These are all very useful strategies for helping teachers to deal with defiant students, but there are some strengths that students with ODD bring to the classroom environment as well, and it's important to recognize them. Students with ODD are able to both learn and pay attention in class just like any other student, and they have a normal memory. But, more so than other students, students with ODD are often highly motivated by the use of rewards for good behavior. They also learn better with practical, hands-on learning methods, and they are very creative, so art is a subject in which they excel. By recognizing these strengths, teachers can tailor lessons to help the student with ODD meet their academic goals and learn proper social skills, as well.

Toward that end, teachers want to work to establish effective classroom interactions. It's important that teachers establish realistic behavioral goals for students suffering from behavioral disorders like ODD. For example, for a student who throws a fit and leaves the room when asked to do something, it would be a realistic goal to just have them stay in the room. Don't expect to turn the behavior around all at once; rather, set realistic goals and work toward improving upon those as you go along. Once the child has improved to the point where they stay in the classroom, you can work on their angry outbursts. As always, teachers should use a combination of positive reinforcement and consistent, predetermined consequences to slowly change a child's behavior.

To monitor those changes, the teacher should collect baseline data when they are first working with the student. How often do they misbehave? Is it 0, 10, 15, or 20 percent of the time? Once you have the baseline data, you can then continue to rate the child's behavior to document progress or lack thereof. You'll have to be patient since it takes time to change those bad behaviors, and as we've noted, you'll want to use plenty of positive reinforcement to do so. This is far more effective than instituting punishments. By praising their positive behavior, you make it the focus of your attention rather than the bad behavior. Be careful, however, about putting students in the spotlight since that can make them feel insecure. Perhaps, talk to them privately or even write your praise so they can enjoy it without feeling embarrassed in front of the classroom.

Teachers also have to monitor their own emotions and reactions carefully so that they don't do more damage than good. You shouldn't assume a student will act badly: wait and see if they do. Take a deep breath to calm yourself and don't intervene unless you absolutely have to do so. If you can avoid a power struggle, that will be the better course of action. Teachers should also not be afraid to reach out for help when they need it. The school counselor is a good place to start. They can observe the classroom, student behavior, and interactions with the teacher, and from there, they can provide tips for helping de-escalate any behavioral problems that arise. Sometimes, they might also want to work with the affected students individually. Commonly, they can help those students to identify triggers and enact a plan of behaviors to use in those situations. Another source of help can come from the school's special education team. They're used to using specialized tactics to help keep things in the classroom calm and on track. They also might be able to work with specific children individually as you engage with the rest of the class.

Another source of frustration for many students with ODD is found in the interactions they have with other students. For that reason, without revealing the specific problems of any one student, it can help if the teacher has a talk with the entire class about handling frustrating feelings. You can explain that what someone finds to be difficult depends on the individual person. What one person finds easy, another finds it to be very difficult. It's also true that some people have an easier time controlling their emotions and others find that to be more difficult. You can then have a class discussion about how to deal with your own frustrating feelings as well as the feelings of other people. You can enlist the entire class in determining what is appropriate behavior in the classroom. This will help them, including your students with ODD, to take ownership of their own environment. You can discuss appropriate actions to take to de-escalate a situation when someone is having difficulty controlling their emotions. It's a great opportunity to teach them about empathy and compassion. This will help bond as a class and take care of each other.

As part of your discussion with the class, have the students help you establish an emotional communication system. You might begin by asking, "How can we let others know when we're about to lose control?" Students might come up with some kind of scale, like 1 - 10, where ten means everything's great and one means I can't take it anymore. Students can all set up numbered cards that they can pass to the teacher or other students to indicate their emotional state. If a student lets you know they're having a bad day, you can arrange to keep things kind of low key. Perhaps, they can read quietly or go to the gym. If it's particularly bad, they might like to visit with the school counselor. If all the students are engaged in this process and know what to do when they feel overly emotional, those students affected with ODD won't feel singled out. They'll have their privacy and help with a solution, too. Additionally, other students will be learning appropriate ways to signal their emotional states as well.

It's a good tactic to make a behavioral contract with the class just like parents might make a similar contract with their own child. This will identify specific behaviors and rewards or consequences for each. Your job will be to ensure the rewards and consequences are reasonable, but with this kind of system, you're engaging the entire classroom community in establishing appropriate behavioral rules they are agreeing to live by. That gives them both agency and ownership in the outcome. It also signals to students affected by disorders like ODD that appropriate behaviors are not only applicable to them, all students and the teacher are expected to conform to the established behavioral contract for their shared environment. That helps the child with ODD develop their social skills and sense of community.

As part of the behavioral contract, you want it to identify specific, measured actions that detail the expectations for student behavior. It will detail helpful ways to de-escalate challenging situations that arise. It will promote more understanding and compassion in dealing with anyone--whether they have ODD or not--who feels they are losing control of their emotions. It's an opportunity to help children put themselves in another person's shoes to try to understand how they are feeling. You can even do exercises designed to elicit empathetic responses. Have students talk about, for example, how frustrating and hurtful it would be if they didn't have a lot of friends. Help them to take a moment and really think about how they would feel in a given situation. Many times, we underestimate kids, but if we give them a chance to show compassion and empathy, they will often surprise us with the depth of their understanding. That can help create long-term friendships for students with ODD who might not otherwise have that in their lives. This can also help you, as the teacher of behaviorally challenged students, to develop a deeper, more understanding relationship with those students.

Providing Support

Bronwyn Harris found out the hard way about ODD. She had never heard of ODD until Antonio walked through the doors of her classroom. Harris had worked with troubled students before, but she wasn't prepared for the level of disruption Antonio displayed. He would say, "No," before she even finished asking him a question. If another student tapped him on the shoulder, he would turn around and physically attack that student. When she found out about ODD, Harris finally understood why she felt helpless and stressed, and she was finally able to start instituting effective strategies to help Antonio control his behavior.

As a teacher, you might never encounter a student with ODD, but it almost goes without saying that you will encounter defiant students from time to time. Understanding these strategies can help you deal with that kind of behavior whether it comes with a diagnosis or not. Disruptive students in general, and ODD students specifically, have problems effectively managing their emotions, find it hard to follow instructions and adhere to rules, often have trouble making and keeping friends because of difficulties communicating and understanding social situations, and they have difficulty with problem-solving. These problems can affect their self-esteem and result in emotional outbursts. During these outbursts, disruptive students are unable to understand how their behavior affects other people, and they don't think about consequences. So, what are the ways in which the teacher can provide support for these students?

We've already mentioned a number of ways to help. These strategies include setting up clear expectations that involve rewards for positive behaviors and consequences for negative ones. The environment should be a positive one that promotes learning and helps students deal with frustrating feelings when they come up. Teachers want to be proactive if they see a child becoming frustrated, and they should keep their voice calm as they attempt to de-escalate the situation. They also want to help build the child's skillset with activities that assist them in learning valuable social skills as well as academic requirements. It will help to have a clear, predictable schedule as students respond well when they know what is going to happen each day. Teachers should provide praise to help build student confidence and motivation. Involving the entire class in practicing empathetic, compassionate responses and developing a community-based contract for behavior can help students afflicted with ODD build friendships and feel a sense of community. Finally, teachers want to collaborate with parents in all of the strategies they use so that there is consistency in the home as well as at school.

With respect to the curriculum, teachers should be aware that students suffering with ODD often have trouble with math, but they are often very creative. The arts is a subject in which they frequently excel and by emphasizing that in their curriculum, it can give them a way to express their emotions, build friendships, and boost their self-esteem. Through various types of arts related courses, they can learn valuable listening and sharing skills. There may also be ways to incorporate other skills as well. For example, if the student excels at drawing, by having them draw something like a blueprint, you can incorporate some math skills into the lesson in a way the student may find more engaging. In short, get creative with the ways you stimulate good behavior, motivation, and learning, and you'll find that teaching students with ODD can be one of the most rewarding challenges of your career. The following offer some examples of strategies you can employ in your classroom.

Examples of Teaching and Instructional Strategies for Children with ODD

These examples illustrate some possible challenges that students with ODD often have in school. With each example, you can see the strategies employed by the teachers to help ODD students manage their behavior and have a better learning experience.

Tony

Tony was a third grade student who had problems with following classroom rules and guidelines. In his math class, Tony constantly talked out of turn and without raising his hand as is the classroom rule. Tony's teacher wanted to implement effective strategies to help Tony learn how to both understand and follow the rules set up for the class. What should the teacher do?

1. Tony's teacher should remember to maintain their composure at all times to avoid triggering a confrontation with Tony.
2. The teacher should also provide Tony with clear expectations for behavior in the classroom. These rules would include the fact that raising one's hand is non-negotiable; the rules should be clearly posted in the classroom for all students to see throughout the day.
3. The consequences for not following the rules should also be provided to Tony in a clear way.
4. If Tony disobeys the clearly provided rules, the teacher should use a calm, quiet voice and make a positive statement to Tony that avoids using the words "stop" or "don't." For example, "Tony, I need you to raise your hand when you want to talk in class. I want to hear what you have to say, but I need you to wait until I call on you so that I can focus on what you're saying."

5. The teacher should also be consistent in administering consequences for breaking the rules. These consequences should be predetermined as part of a behavior plan established by the teacher along with Tony's parents.

Erica

Erica is in the second grade, and she has a tendency to distract other students and begin unprovoked fights with them. These distractions are negatively impacting the learning of other students in the classroom. Erica's teacher would like to develop and implement a plan to help Erica stop fighting with other students or distracting them from their learning process. What should Erica's teacher do?

1. Talk to the entire class about the importance of walking away from confrontations to help calm situations down.
2. Place Erica near the front of the class where the teacher can see her behavior, and post clear rules for everyone about respecting other people's learning process.
3. Model the appropriate social behavior after providing Erica with clear expectations for appropriate interactions with fellow classmates and predetermined consequences for failing to do so.
4. Integrate cooperative lessons that build social skills into the curriculum. This will help students learn appropriate ways of interacting with others.
5. Provide Erica with a cool-down area where she can go to be alone when she feels frustrated with other students. The area should be free of any distractions and provide her with outlets for her strong emotions--like pillows to throw or hug or a tactile bin for calming down.

Michael

Michael is in the sixth grade. He frequently has angry outbursts while in class. He also has unprovoked tantrums that involve obscene, hurtful language toward both peers and teachers. Michael believes winning is important and he is commonly spiteful in these negative interactions. His teacher believes his outbursts hurt the learning environment for other students, and she is also fearful for the safety of others. What should Michael's teacher do?

1. Attempt to identify and avoid triggers for Michael's behavior.
2. Talk to the entire class about the importance of avoiding confrontations and behaving appropriately.
3. Create a cool-down area for Michael where he can be alone and release his anger as necessary.
4. Work with Michael on deep-breathing exercises and other techniques he can use to calm down.
5. Avoid power struggles with Michael so he won't feel he has control of the teacher.
6. Meet with school administrators and Michael's parents to create a behavioral support plan that will provide a comfortable atmosphere for Michael to use to implement specific actions for controlling his emotions. This plan should also outline both goals and outlines for Michael's behavior in the classroom.

Angela

Angela is in the fifth grade. She consistently refuses to complete her assigned schoolwork. She frequently either ignores instructions or pretends not to understand them. She has trouble admitting the difficulties she has, and she tends to blame her shortcomings on others. Angela's teacher wants to motivate her so she will complete her assigned schoolwork. What should Angela's teacher do?

1. The first thing to do is make sure that the assigned work is appropriate for Angela's academic level.

2. Involve Angela more in the learning process by giving her choices. These can be as simple as where to sit while she is working or it can involve choosing how she presents her work. This will help her feel like she has some control over her own learning.
3. Allow Angela to redo assignments she has not completed or not completed satisfactorily.
4. Intersperse preferred activities between non-preferred activities. This provides a small reward for Angela if she completes a non-preferred activity. Set up the work as a series of goals with Angela's input, and make sure you use proper incentives for completing each goal.
5. Maintain the normal routines in the classroom so that Angela will feel comfortable listening to instructions and completing the assignments.

Teaching Conflict Resolution Skills

Another great thing that teachers can do for any student, but particularly for those students with disruptive behavioral disorders, is to teach conflict resolution skills. It's helpful since many students lack the basic skills for resolving common conflicts whether with other students, adults, or other authority figures. When you give them the proper skills for resolving conflicts, you're empowering the students to be more independent in their lives by solving at least some of their own problems. For the teacher, it means having to intervene less frequently as students are able to solve minor conflicts and that increases the instructional time in the classroom. Resolving conflicts is also something that promotes maturity. Students learn social skills for navigating in an adult world. This will also improve their self-confidence, and it will also reduce instances of tattling and classroom disruptions.

Teaching conflict resolution skills is a great way to begin the school year, and it should be repeated to varying degrees once a month to make sure the strategies are fresh in student's minds. The strategies can also be reviewed anytime that students are arguing a lot in class or if the teacher finds they are losing time because of conflicts and disagreements. It's something that's important to go over if a student has been suspended due to fighting or conflicts with students and adults, and it's also helpful when students have problems compromising, sharing, or taking turns.

Conflict resolution skills can be taught at different levels or tiers. Tier 1 conflict resolution would involve the whole class or group. Tier 2 would be instituted for conflict interventions between individuals or groups having specific problems, and Tier 3 would involve customized lessons for specific students. There are many different strategies that can be used for this, but a few examples are provided here that can be used for individual students, small groups, or the whole class. Remember that these skills should be reviewed and practiced on a regular basis. If students are involved in a conflict and fail to use the skills they've learned, it's helpful to have the student(s) reflect on how they might have handled it better. As always, the teacher should model the behavior they are teaching the students.

The following activities are written in language that is appropriate to share with your students:

ACTIVITY #1: DISCUSSION QUESTIONS

Give the students time to answer each of the following questions either alone or working in small groups, then open it up for the entire class to discuss their answers.

1. Describe a disagreement, argument, or fight you've had with someone.
2. How did this conflict end?
3. How did you feel about the conflict and about how it ended?
4. Why do you think disagreements or arguments can sometimes be helpful?

5. Why is it important for people involved in conflicts to talk and listen to each other?
6. Why is it important that you share your feelings rather than keep them inside yourself?

Activity #2: Fairy Tale Conflicts

Objectives: After completing this activity, students will be able to:

- Accurately identify feelings and needs inherent in conflicts.
- Develop creative solutions for cooperatively resolving conflict.

The approximate time for the activity is 45 minutes.

Activity Instructions: Fairy tales always have some kind of conflict. Goldilocks broke into the bears' house; the Big Bad Wolf destroyed the pigs' property; Cinderella was treated terribly by her stepmother. So, someone has to help these characters resolve their conflicts in a healthier way! Choose a fairy tale to examine and while reading it, think about the conflicts involved in the story. Then, answer the following questions:

1. What is the conflict presented in the story?
2. How do the main characters feel about the conflict in the story?
3. What does each character want or need to resolve the conflict?

Make a list of three possible solutions that would resolve the conflict to the benefit of everyone. These are fairy tales, so feel free to be as creative as you like.

You can enhance this activity by then having students select their favorite solution and rewrite the ending of the fairy tale to show how the characters worked together to solve the conflict. You can also have students share and compare their solutions with their classmates. They can discuss which solution is the most creative, which is the most likely to work, and which would make each of the characters the happiest.

You can then have students reflect on a conflict in their own lives and come up with one way to resolve that conflict or at least deal with their feelings in a healthier way. Have them make goals for themselves for controlling their anger in a healthier way the next time it happens. They can even write a brief essay about a situation where they were able to express and control their anger.

Activity #3: Conflict Corner

Objective: After completing this activity, students will be able to identify strategies for managing and resolving various types of conflicts.

Instructions: Conflict Corner is an online chat group for middle students. They share their conflicts and the hosts of the chat help them solve their problems. This week, you're the guest host, and you'll be giving advice to students about how to handle their conflicts. Students have already posted their problems, so you can take time to prepare your response. Read the conflicts below and choose one of these students to help. Write a response to the student that includes the following information:

1. A clear description of the conflict
2. Reasons why it's important to resolve conflicts
3. At least two suggestions for resolving the conflict.

Conflict Sample Scenarios:

Student 1

Katie writes: My math teacher, Mrs. Miller, is really mean to me! She gives us way too much work to do, and she never has any fun activities for us to do. Also, when you get an answer wrong in her class, she sometimes makes kids cry. No matter what I do, Mrs. Miller is never going to like me. That makes me feel like why should I bother doing anymore work in her class? She's going to pick on me no matter what, so what difference does it make if I just don't do the work?

Student 2

Ryan writes: My sister is such a big baby, and my parents give her so much attention. Sometimes I feel like I'm not even a member of the family. I've been waiting a whole year to get a new gaming system, but she gets what she wants when she wants it. Also, when we go on a trip, we have to go somewhere for babies so she can go on the little kid's rides. I don't want to be around her at all anymore, so whenever she comes around me, I just go to my room and shut the door.

Student 3

Luke writes: You think your parents are mean? Mine won't even let me watch any more than one hour of TV a day! I can't believe it. They also won't let me go to the movies with my friends on Saturday. Last time they told me I couldn't do something, I just snuck out of the house and did it anyway. I got in trouble, but I don't care anymore. I'm just going to do what I want.

Student 4

Hannah writes: I don't want to go to school anymore. I know Penny is going to say something horrible about me in front of everyone. Last week, she tripped me in the cafeteria and I fell on my lunch tray. Then, she spent all day making fun of me. She says the meanest things to hurt my feelings. Now, even some of my friends don't want to hang out with me anymore because they're afraid Penny will start picking on them.

After students complete this activity, you can have them share their resolutions to the conflicts they chose. Take that opportunity to have students discuss other conflicts as well.

CHAPTER SUMMARY

In this chapter, we've discussed strategies teachers can use in the classroom to help manage the behavior of students with ODD. Specifically, we've covered the following topics:

- Behavioral strategies teachers can employ in their interactions with students.
- Classroom strategies teachers can employ to help manage the behavior of all students, particularly those with ODD.
- How teachers can gain a deeper understanding and provide support for students with ODD.
- Examples of teaching and instructional strategies to employ.
- Teaching conflict resolution.

IN THE NEXT CHAPTER YOU WILL LEARN ABOUT THE COMMON DISORDERS that co-occur with ODD.

7

CO-OCCURRING DISORDERS WITH ODD

When two or more disorders occur simultaneously, they are called comorbidities or are said to co-occur. For ODD, there are several comorbidities that occur most commonly. Among these are ADHD, other disruptive behavioral disorders, substance abuse, generalized anxiety disorder, depression, and even Tourette syndrome. It's important to understand the various disorders that might occur with ODD since the symptoms may overlap. To choose the best treatment options, you need a full understanding of all disorders that might affect your child. Let's take a look at each of these comorbidities to gain a better understanding of these various disorders.

ATTENTION DEFICIT HYPERACTIVITY DISORDER

ADHD is a common comorbidity with ODD. In one study (Biederman et al., 1996), the comorbidity of ADHD and ODD was 46 percent for children as young as 6-years-old and 33 percent for adolescents. Chen et al. (2013) also found that girls with ADHD were less likely to develop comorbid ODD than boys; however, when disruptive behavior disorders like ODD are comorbid with ADHD, they have a poorer prognosis than when they occur alone regardless of gender. The co-occurrence of ODD and ADHD may be explained by some common genetic factors as well as nonshared environmental factors that can affect both disorders (Thapar et al., 2001).

Studies have also shown that patients with ODD and comorbid ADHD as well as those with ODD alone have deficits in their visuospatial working memory. That indicates that the deficits are an underlying factor in the ODD rather than the ADHD (Saarinen et al., 2014). Your visuospatial working memory is critical for depth perception and movement as it helps you identify, integrate, and analyze spatial and visual details and structure so that you can navigate around objects as you move. Your memory comes in as it helps you recall and manipulate images your eyes are receiving so that you can remain oriented spatially and you can keep track of moving objects. People with deficits in this system might have trouble driving because they have problems judging distance correctly, and they can also have problems navigating through spaces. They might, for example, have a tendency to bump into things.

CONDUCT DISORDER (CD)

There is a definite association between ODD and CD, but researchers disagree on the nature of that association. Some believe that ODD and CD are discrete disorders that follow divergent courses with ODD being relatively benign and having a good prognosis and CD being the more severe disorder. Other researchers, however, believe the two disorders as well as ADHD are all part of the same disorder, but just represent varying degrees of severity. These experts would argue that ADHD symptoms can progress to ODD which, in turn, can progress to CD. Moreover, researchers have identified two subtypes of ODD. One is prodromal to CD, meaning it is the early form of CD, and another that is subsyndromal to CD, meaning it is part of the same disorder, but a milder form that is not likely to progress into CD (Ghosh & Sinha, 2012).

In one study (Ghosh & Sinha), meaningful distinctions were identified between ADHD, ODD, and CD, but because of their shared risk factors--genetic, environmental, or a combination of the two--these researchers concluded that the three disorders were part of the same psychopathological spectrum. They noted in particular the high degree of overlapping symptoms that include aggression, hostility, and emotionality. Thus, these behavioral disorders may not only be comorbidities, they may actually be different levels of severity of the same disorder.

Substance Abuse

There are several studies that identified an increased risk for various behavioral disorders, including ODD, and substance abuse. One study (Rodgers et al., 2014) on more than 238 children examined subjects with ADHD, ODD, and CD, all of whom were diagnosed before 15-years-old, found that CD had the highest association with substance abuse, and that subtype was followed by one that included those children who had multiple comorbidities as opposed to a single disorder. Children with ADHD showed elevated frequencies for alcohol abuse. Because of ODD's close association as a prodromal subtype for CD, there exists a significant risk for substance abuse if the milder disorder continues to progress into CD.

It's not surprising that children who experience problems regulating their own emotions could develop problems with substance abuse later in life. Disruptive behavioral disorders create stressful emotional feelings that cause many people to self-medicate. Given the emotional turmoil created by their disorder, it's understandable they would seek ways to feel better. That's why intervening at a young age is critical so that these children can learn to manage their emotions and self-regulate without the need for substances like alcohol or drugs.

Generalized Anxiety Disorder (GAD)

Despite the fact that ODD is comorbid with numerous behavioral disorders, there is still a paucity of research into the co-occurrence of ODD with generalized anxiety disorder. The research that has been done has shown that ODD in combination with an anxiety disorder leads to a reluctance to engage with other people which has important implications for your child's social skills. ODD patients with comorbid GAD are also less likely to comply with treatment plans, and that can lead to a worsening of both disorders. Added to that is the fact that parents of children with both disorders report that their child's defiant behavior is especially difficult to manage. Still, the research has mostly focused on combined multiple disruptive behavioral disorders like those described above for ADHD and CD. That makes it difficult to parse the specific relationship between ODD and GAD (Drabick et al., 2008).

The research does show, however, that GAD and ODD are comorbid across various developmental stages of life. Those children who enter preschool with persistent ODD, for example, are at risk for developing an anxiety disorder. The highest risk, however, occurs in middle childhood and decreases during adolescence. It appears that it is the presence of ODD that predicts for the development of anxiety rather than the other way around. There is, however, a risk in adolescents who suffer from anxiety for developing ODD. Moreover, both of these disorders are associated with the development of other psychological problems like CD, major depressive disorder (MDD), and substance abuse. That makes it important to conduct more research into the comorbidity of ODD and GAD. One study involving 243 6- to 10-year olds found additional support for the comorbidity of these disorders. Drabick et al. (2008) specifically found that comorbid ODD and GAD were associated with those children living in homes with high levels of familial conflict. They also found that the constraints of the classroom may minimize the display of symptoms as compared to the home environment. That illustrates the importance of using more than one source to identify children who are in the most need of intervention.

It also appears there may be differences in the way that children's symptoms are interpreted. For example, it's possible that children who have trouble establishing healthy peer relationships are perceived by their mothers as anxious, but their teachers interpret their behavior as oppositional. The latter may be due to the fact that many children are reluctant to talk about emotional and social problems with teachers. This presents a possible problem with the studies that have been conducted to date. Namely, are there genuine comorbidities here or are the apparent differences in symptoms merely reflective of differences in the interpretation of the child's behavior? The teacher calls it defiant and the parents see anxiety or vice versa. This could have important implications since different environmental constraints could affect the ultimate diagnosis and subsequent recommended treatment interventions. Research (Drabick et al., 2008) has shown that the symptoms exhibited by a child were associated with different problems by different informants. That shows that one informant is not the same as another, and thus, the different observations must be placed in their proper context to truly make an appropriate diagnosis. This is further complicated by the consideration of other possible comorbidities like ADHD. ADHD symptoms further obscure the relationship of ODD to GAD as well as create more difficulty with identifying consistent symptoms among informants.

Major Depressive Disorder (MDD)

Perhaps the age group at greatest risk for developing depression in association with ODD is that of adolescence. Depression by itself is common in this age range, and it is also frequently associated with numerous behavioral, emotional, and social problems. Some studies have demonstrated a prevalence of 7 to 8 percent for depressive disorders in adolescents. These are often associated with externalizing behaviors. For ODD, prevalence rates between 3.2 and 13.3 percent have been identified for adolescent boys. For adolescent girls with ODD, the rates range from between 1.4 and 9.4 percent. The rates of CD run between 1.8 and 8.7 percent for this age range. The research has also shown that depression and behavioral disorders frequently co-occur, and this has serious implications for public health. One study showed some 70 percent of adolescent suicide victims met the criteria established for both a mood disorder like depression and an externalizing disorder like ODD (Jacobs et al., 2010).

Regardless of whether the full criteria for either are met, many adolescents who are seen at the clinic display mixed symptoms. There are some shared features of depression and ODD and both can result in the functional impairment of the child's life caused by numerous challenging behaviors. These include poor social skills, poor peer relationships, and problematic behavior at school. The internalizing and externalizing factors in both ODD and depression are correlated. ODD exhibits three dimensions in adolescents: irritable, headstrong, and hurtful, and these work to impair the lives of these young people. They prevent them from forming positive peer relationships, and they keep them from performing well in school. All of that is correlated with MDD, and there are strong associations between ODD in adolescents and psychopathology in adult life. Thus, the patterns of behavior begun at this age carry forward into adulthood if the proper interventions are not implemented (Jacobs et al., 2010).

Jacobs et al. (2010) found that effective treatments for depression were helpful in reducing symptoms of ODD to subclinical levels. The treatments they researched that showed the most promise were those that included a medication component, namely fluoxetine and serotonin reuptake inhibitors. They concluded that the results were in line with the concept known as dynamic comorbidity. This is where changes in the conduct disorders in children paralleled changes in depression. The less the child was depressed, the less they showed symptoms associated with conduct disorders. Given this, the treatment of depression is paramount for treating comorbid disruptive behavioral disorders. The researchers also identified several core processes that appear to represent general risk factors for both MDD and ODD. These include a negative self-image, low self-worth, familial risk factors like conflict and self-regulation problems, to name a few. The correlated risk factors and overlapping symptoms have led them to propose the possibility that ODD is a specific subtype of depression. In adults, there are distinct psychological and neuroendocrine (i.e. hormonal) profiles in those individuals who present with symptoms of hostile depression, though more research is needed to adequately describe the overlapping processes.

Tourette Syndrome (TS)

Tourette Syndrome is a condition that affects the nervous system and results in tics. Tics are sudden movements, twitches, or sounds that people do repetitively. These tics are not under the control of the person affected by this condition. They cannot stop themselves from doing these things. They might grunt unwillingly or blink repetitively or make certain sounds over and over again. In fact, the person is compelled to do the tic, even if they can resist for a while. The types of tics can be put in two general categories: motor and vocal.

Motor tics include movements of the body like blinking, shrugging, or jerking body parts. Vocal tics include any sound that the person can make with their voice. Examples include humming, yelling out words or phrases, or clearing the throat. Moreover, tics can be simple or complicated. Simple ones would be moving a few body parts like squinting repeatedly or sniffing. Complex tics involve many different body parts that often move in a pattern. For example, someone who suffers from TS might bob their head while simultaneously jerking their arm, and those actions could be followed by jumping in the air. These behaviors typically begin between five and ten years of age. The earliest symptoms are motor tics in the head and neck. They tend to get worse when the child is excited or stressed, and they improve when he or she is calm and focused on some kind of activity.

The tics typically will decrease during adolescence and into early adulthood. Sometimes they disappear altogether, but there are many people who still suffer with TS into later adulthood. In fact, in some cases, the symptoms can become worse in adulthood. Although you might have seen this disorder portrayed in film and other media with people spontaneously calling out swear words--a symptom called coprolalia--that is a rare symptom. It is not even required for a diagnosis.

Tourette syndrome is frequently comorbid with other conditions, including ADHD, ODD, OCD, MDD, GAD, autism, and other learning disorders. In fact, most children who are diagnosed with TS have at least one other mental health, behavioral, or developmental condition. The research suggests that people with TS are at higher risk for behavioral and social problems, as you might imagine. The high frequency of comorbidity in children diagnosed with TS necessitates a careful medical assessment to arrive at the correct diagnosis. This can be difficult because of overlapping symptoms like rage.

Some people who suffer from TS experience anger that is out of control. These are called episodes of rage. This is also a symptom of various behavioral disorders including ADHD, ODD, and CD. One of the subtle differences is that with behavioral disorders, rage happens repeatedly and is way out of line with the trigger. For those children affected by TS, the episodes of rage tend to happen at home rather than outside the home, and like the behavioral disorders, these episodes include yelling, cursing, kicking, hitting, biting, and throwing objects. As with ODD and other behavioral disorders, the treatment includes learning self-regulation behaviors, extensive training in social skills, and the implementation of relaxation techniques. While some of the treatments are similar, it is still necessary to identify any comorbidities to implement full treatment interventions.

BIPOLAR DISORDER

Bipolar disorder is a mental condition that causes extreme mood and behavioral changes. It used to be called manic-depressive illness or manic depression, and it results in moods that are polar opposites. A child or adult with this disorder may feel extremely happy one moment and incredibly depressed the next. The 'happy' moods are referred to as manic episodes. They may not be characterized by happiness, per se; these episodes are marked, rather, by an increase in energy and activity more so than a happy mood. The other side of the coin is depression and low activity levels. This is called a depressive episode.

Bipolar disorder is not the same thing as the normal ups and downs of childhood. These mood changes are much more extreme, are unprovoked, and are often accompanied by other symptoms like changes in sleep patterns, energy levels, and the ability to focus mentally and think clearly. As you have probably guessed, these symptoms make it hard for children to concentrate in school and get along with both friends and family members. Additionally, the depressive episodes can be so extreme that some children and teens affected by this disorder attempt suicide.

Most people are diagnosed with this disorder in their adolescence or early adulthood, but symptoms can begin in childhood. The disorder is episodic but long-lasting. It usually lasts for an individual's entire life. As with many of the other comorbidities we've examined, there are numerous overlapping symptoms with bipolar disorder and behavioral disorders like ODD.

There are high rates of comorbid ODD and BPD as indicated by various studies. The frequency of co-occurring ODD in individuals with BPD are as high as 47 - 88 percent. Comorbidity is not as high for BPD in individuals suffering from ODD, however. Only about 20 percent of children with ODD are found to also have comorbid BPD. In fact, ODD is described as the second most common comorbidity with BPD, second only to ADHD. The diagnosis is challenging since there are numerous overlapping symptoms. It can be difficult to distinguish ODD from the manic episodes associated with BPD. The research also suggests the possibility of different subtypes of ODD as it relates to BPD with one subtype being a distinct disorder and another that may be prodromal to BPD. More research is needed to determine if that is the case (Joshi & Wilens, 2009).

As you can see by now, there are numerous comorbidities with ODD. These include other behavioral disorders as well as mood disorders. The high frequency of comorbidities indicates the need for more research and careful examination to arrive at the appropriate diagnosis. It's important to determine the proper treatment interventions as well as for the better understanding of the reasons behind your child's problematic behaviors. It's also critical for your child's future that you have a complete understanding of the behavioral disorders and any mood disorders they have.

Chapter Summary

In this chapter, we've discussed the various comorbid disorders that occur with ODD. Specifically, we've covered the following topics:

- The definition of a comorbidity
- The co-occurrence of ADHD with ODD
- Conduct disorder and ODD
- Substance abuse and ODD
- Generalized anxiety disorder and ODD
- Major depressive disorder and ODD
- Comorbid Tourette syndrome
- Bipolar disorder and ODD

In the next chapter you will learn about the occurrence of ODD in adults.

8

OPPOSITIONAL DEFIANT DISORDER IN ADULTS

Oppositional Defiant Disorder is not just a problem in children. While it is more common in children, it is also seen in adults, and it can have a devastating effect on their lives. They also share similar symptoms as seen in children with this disorder.

Adults with these symptoms:

- Frequently lose their temper
- Often argue with family members and coworkers
- Purposefully defy or refuse to comply with laws or rules
- Deliberately seek to annoy people
- Blame others for their mistakes
- Feel easily annoyed by others
- Are angry and resentful most of the time
- Act out in spiteful or vindictive ways

Because these symptoms are occurring in adults, they may manifest in slightly different ways depending on the environment. In the home, an adult with ODD may present as an overly argumentative spouse or a hostile roommate. They will always need to win any argument in which they participate, will constantly be fighting any authority figures, might do things like leave clothes on the floor just to purposely annoy those with whom they are living, and might find themselves cited by the police for disorderly conduct on a regular basis. These are also individuals who frequently get involved in physical altercations like bar fights, and they become enraged with the slightest provocation.

In the work environment, ODD may manifest as nearly constant arguments with coworkers and supervisors. These individuals will feel oppressed by the rules in the workplace. Moreover, these individuals will seek ways to annoy their coworkers. For example, they might eat particularly strong smelling foods for lunch if they realize it is irritating to those around them. These people often get fired for physical aggression against coworkers in heated arguments. They also are the ones who will have meltdowns during a meeting or performance review where they receive even the mildest constructive criticism.

As with children, these symptoms should persist for at least six months and include at least four of the symptoms listed above before looking for a diagnosis. These symptoms often manifest as verbal abuse or fits of rage as might be seen in cases of road rage. These are people who are very aggressive and deliberately irritating. They often express being angry at the world for no good reason, and their temper is on a hair trigger. They will also typically describe themselves as misunderstood, disliked, penned in, and/or pushed around.

Adults who constantly oppose authority figures also have difficulty keeping a steady job as well as maintaining their personal relationships. They are quick to anger, impatient, and have a low tolerance for frustration. They typically consider themselves to be victims of injustice or unfair treatment in their own family. They will describe themselves as being the subject of mistreatment, and they feel misunderstood and unappreciated.

CAUSES OF ODD IN ADULTS

ODD typically has its onset in childhood. Without effective treatment, it can simply persist into adulthood. While some children will outgrow their ODD--usually by age eight or nine--approximately one-half will experience symptoms into adulthood. As we discussed for children, ODD has a strong genetic component: it often runs in families where several family members might be affected. Adults who still report symptoms of ODD report being angry all of the time, and approximately 40 percent of these individuals will continue to get progressively worse. The problem can even evolve into antisocial personality disorder.

Many adults with ODD also suffer from ADHD. In fact, 45 to 84 percent of children with untreated ADHD symptoms will develop ODD as well. That has led some experts to speculate that the problems with emotional regulation that are evident with ADHD might also lead to ODD. If the situation goes untreated, these adults have persistent problems with conflict in their professional and personal life.

Treatment for ODD in Adults

As with children, treatment for ODD in adults often focuses on helping them to develop better strategies for managing their emotions. Anger management is a common type of therapy that seeks to help these individuals improve their interpersonal relationships at home and in the workplace. They are taught strategies for managing their feelings of defiance as well as ways to set goals for making positive changes and overcoming those intense emotions they so often feel. Therapists will also work with their families, spouses, partners, and friends to help them improve communication skills as well as understand better how ODD affects their loved one. This can help everyone concerned bring more harmony to the relationship. Medications are also commonly prescribed. In adults, many of the same stimulant medications that help treat ADHD are also effective for ODD.

It is important to note that adults and adolescents with ODD are at a 90 percent greater risk of being diagnosed with another mental illness in their lifetime. This speaks to the cumulative nature of ODD.

People who suffer from ODD are also at a greater risk for substance abuse and suicide. That's why it's critical to intervene early in the development of the disorder. The ramifications of living with untreated ODD are serious, and can cause lifelong problems in every aspect of an individual's life.

Chapter Summary

In this chapter, we've discussed the manifestation of ODD in adults. Specifically, we've discussed the following topics:

- The general symptoms of ODD in adults.
- The symptoms that manifest in the personal life of an adult with ODD.
- The symptoms that manifest in the professional life of an adult with ODD.
- The causes of ODD in adults.
- Treatment strategies for adults with ODD.

In the next chapter you will learn about several case studies of children with ODD.

9

CASE STUDIES IN ODD

This chapter presents several documented case studies of children diagnosed with ODD. These are offered as a demonstration of the various manifestations of the disorder, the diagnostic techniques employed, and the efficacy of treatment regimens used in these cases. The most important thing to take from these is that there is hope for your child. If they are carefully diagnosed and treated early, there is no reason they can't go on to live normal, productive, and happy lives.

CASE STUDY #1: MARY

Mary is the 4-year-old daughter of parents who are both active-duty military officers. Neither of Mary's parents have a history of mental illness or substance abuse. Mary's mother initially brought her into the child psychiatry clinic after noticing that she had started to withhold her bowel movements. She was also becoming more defiant at home and this was manifesting in the form of frequent temper tantrums.

The doctor began by inquiring about recent stressors in her family life. Mary's mother revealed that her husband had been geographically separated from the family since Mary was 3½ years old. They visited him one a month where he was stationed in another state. Mary's mother reported that the problematic behavior had begun relatively soon after the child's father had moved. The family was temporarily reunited after three months of living apart, but during that three month period, Mary's behavior showed no improvement.

Four months before Mary had her 4th birthday, she started preschool. It was a month after that that she began to withhold her bowel movements. A few short weeks after that, Mary's father was deployed to Bosnia. Regarding the child's toilet training, Mary's mother told the doctor that she had been easy to train around the age of two. Though she trained easily, she still wore a diaper to bed since she would sometimes urinate in her sleep.

Once Mary began withholding her bowel movements, she began to suffer from constipation and would sometimes leak stool into her underwear during the day. She had been examined by a medical doctor, who had ruled out any physical or medical cause for her symptoms. That doctor had prescribed Milk of Magnesia and mineral oil to treat the constipation. This did help, but she continued to willfully withhold her bowel movements, and therefore, she continued to have problems with stool leakage during the day.

Mary also had a 7 month history of controlling and defiant behavior problems. Arguments with her mother often escalated to temper tantrums during which Mary would throw toys around. These temper tantrums predated the withholding of bowel movements by several months.

Upon examination, the child did not have any evidence of a mood disorder or any kind of developmental delay. Mary was a very verbal child, and her mother reported she had many friends both in her neighborhood and at school. She also did not demonstrate problems related to separation when her mother would drop her off at school, nor did she act out behaviorally while at school though she did continue to withhold bowel movements while there. Mary also got along well with her 6-year-old sister.

During therapy sessions, Mary had difficulty verbalizing her feelings regarding the separation from her father, but that was something to be expected given her age and level of development. When she was asked directly whether she missed her father or not, she would simply smile and say, "No." Mary's mother reported, however, that she was very close with her father right up until he had to move away.

Play therapy was implemented and helped Mary to verbalize her sadness through the characters she made up. Mary's mother also implemented a reward system at home for bowel movements over the course of approximately 10 weeks. Through the concurrent play therapy sessions where Mary was able to express feelings of loss, her withholding of bowel movements resolved, though her controlling and defiant behavior with her mother persisted.

Mary would tell her mother what to eat and drink as well as what clothes to wear. She would also order her to get off the phone, and if her mother refused to comply, Mary would throw a tantrum. This controlling behavior was confined to her mother; she never attempted to control her father, her sister, or her peers. Mary's mother reported that she was not consistent in responding to Mary demands. She said that if they were out in public, she would often comply to avoid a public temper tantrum. Mary's mother was instructed to be consistent with her response to Mary and to implement a time-out regardless of whether they were in public or at home. Over the course of the next several months, the newly implemented strategies lessened Mary's misbehavior. She still continued, however, to be defiant with her mother at home.

While Mary was able to express her feelings of sadness through play therapy, she never verbalized her feelings if she was asked directly about them. She also never spoke to her mother about her feelings. In fact, when her mother would tell her that her father would not be able to come home for the holidays, Mary didn't seem upset at all nor did she express any sad feelings. When asked about how she felt directly, she replied that it was, "Alright." But, in play therapy, she told another doll that families should be together during the holidays.

The pattern Mary demonstrated of being able to express her feelings through play therapy prompted the recommendation that Mary's mother engage in 30 minutes of unstructured play with Mary each day. During that time, Mary could dictate the form and theme of the play. That provided her with some regularly scheduled time each day where she could completely control the interactions she had with adults, and it would allow her to express her feelings. Within several weeks of implementing this play time, Mary showed a dramatic decrease in her controlling behavior towards her mother.

CASE STUDY #2: JL

JL's mother reported that her defiant behaviors began around the age of 3 or 4. The behaviors appeared to be instigated by attempts to emulate her mother. Her mother reported that JL would follow her around as she was doing her housekeeping chores and rearrange furniture, table settings, and knick-knacks in what JL's mother regarded as a means to get attention. Her mother would admonish her for this behavior, and that would trigger the defiance that later became a part of JL's emotional personality.

JL's parents later divorced, and JL went to live with her father. This cut off any means of resolving the emotional issues she had with her mother. Thus, JL's defiant behavior persisted and resulted in difficulties at school and with forming friendships. In her late teens, JL's mother took up with a new partner. As an academic, he was struck by the difficulty JL had educationally and with attracting suitable young men. She was quite attractive, and yet, she continued to have problems in that regard. JL went on to take courses in nursing at the local community college, but she still had difficulty with her coursework. She complained that her teachers didn't pay enough attention to her.

At school, she met many young men, but none of her romantic relationships lasted. When she was 21-years-old, her parents sent her to Spain to learn Spanish during the summer and to travel around Europe. JL struggled to learn the language and only made one friend. Moreover, she did very little traveling and rebuffed the advances of a young Spanish policeman she met. A few years later, she again enrolled in a nursing program, but continued to have great difficulty with her educational goals. She consistently complained she did not get enough guidance from her teachers. She eventually failed and was unable to remedy her academic standing as a result.

JL had been diagnosed previously with co-dependency and depression, but her new stepfather had done work in a state hospital and had doubted the validity of the depression diagnosis. When he saw a program about ODD, he immediately recognized it as an appropriate description of JL's behavioral problems. When he presented his thoughts to JL, she was initially upset, but kept the information he gave her about ODD. Over the course of several months, her life began to improve dramatically. She was in a better mood, and finally found a good man to be with; in fact, they are still happily together.

JL's stepfather believes she was able to effect a self-cure for the disorder she had suffered from for 40 years. Perhaps, it is because the disorder is more easily recognizable than the other problems with which JL had previously been diagnosed. That may have given her the impetus she needed to take more control over her anger and to stop blaming others for her mistakes.

CASE STUDY #3: GERALD

Gerald was 12-years-old when he was brought to play therapy by a foster parent. He was sweet and cooperative some of the time, but he often manifested defiant behaviors such as talking rudely to adults, breaking rules on purpose, sneaking out of the house, and speaking in an angry manner to his peers and other people around him. He also refused to do his chores. Gerald's foster mother reported that his biological mother had neglected him and he had been in several foster homes. His current foster family wanted to adopt him, but were worried that they would not be able to manage his defiant behavior which was getting worse.

Gerald's therapist initiated play therapy that included art projects, games, and toy army battles. Once the therapist established a good relationship with Gerald, his foster parents were included in the sessions. Gerald was encouraged in these sessions to draw, write, or talk about the experiences he had in other foster homes. He was also encouraged to express these experiences through performance art such as with puppet shows or plays involving the people in the room. Through this expressive art and play therapy, Gerald was able to express his feelings and learn to trust his foster parents. After that, his anger became much more manageable.

Case Study #4: Alice

Alice's ODD behaviors manifested as a wild high school senior. At 17-years-old, she was staying out past curfew, cutting classes, refusing to eat meals with the family, and using drugs. She frequently shouted and swore at her parents if they would try to speak to her or discipline her for her behavior. Her behavior had gone on for eight months during her senior year in high school.

Alice's parents finally decided to seek out a therapist, but Alice refused to go. Her parents were at their wit's end. They don't want to emancipate her, but they don't know how much longer they could put up with her behavior. The therapist decided to explore their relationship, the family history, and their parenting style in an effort to help them manage their own stress and intimacy issues which had been long-standing.

After several weeks of therapy for Alice's parents, they reported that some aspects of her behavior had improved. In fact, she agreed to enter therapy, and during therapy sessions, Alice's parents became more aware of how they had sent her mixed messages with their own behavior. Once Alice felt more understood, her behavior steadily improved.

These four different case studies demonstrate the varied ways in which ODD can manifest. They also show the efficacy of play therapy for younger children and family therapy for older children. One, JL, also offers a cautionary tale. Although JL was eventually able to overcome her ODD symptoms, she spent much of her life living with unresolved anger and defiant behaviors. The proper diagnosis of her symptoms at an earlier stage in her life might have spared her years of disappointment and solitude. It shows the importance of early and careful diagnostic procedures to identify the primary disorder and any existing comorbidities. Still, each story offers hope for anyone suffering from this disorder and their family. There is help, and proper treatment can change lives.

Chapter Summary

In this chapter, we've discussed four case studies of ODD. Specifically, we've talked about the following case studies:

- Mary, whose ODD set in at an early age and was triggered by separation from her father.
- JL whose ODD went undiagnosed for 40 years, but she was able to self-cure once she understood the problem.
- Gerald, a 12-year-old whose ODD was helped by using various forms of art to express his feelings.
- Alice, a 17-year-old who was helped when her parents began to resolve some of their own problems.

The next chapter will present some final words.

FINAL WORDS

Oppositional Defiant Disorder (ODD) can be a devastating behavioral disorder if it goes undiagnosed and untreated. It often sets in early in life, around 4-years-old, when children experience normal defiance as they are exploring their world. ODD, however, is beyond normal defiance. Children afflicted with this disorder throw temper tantrums, talk back to adults, are aggressive and hostile with peers, and are disobedient in school. They have difficulties forming friendships and they suffer academically as well.

Left untreated, ODD can seriously affect the quality of life for those afflicted, and there's evidence that at least some types of ODD can progress into more serious conduct disorders. That can result in substance abuse problems and debilitating depression. Treating a child with ODD can be a challenging endeavor that requires both behavioral and environmental modifications to minimize defiant behaviors. But, with a clear understanding of the symptoms and possibility for comorbid conditions, treatment can be very successful. Children and adults alike can recover and go on to live normal, happy lives.

As with many disorders, the key is in early diagnosis and the implementation of successful and consistent treatment strategies.

That's often easier said than done, however, as the diagnosis of the condition can be complicated by comorbid conditions that include such behavioral disorders as ADHD, CD, as well as mood disorders such as bipolar disorder and major depressive disorder. The fact that some research suggests that many of these disorders may be part of a single psychopathological spectrum only serves to further complicate the matter.

Still, no matter what age or developmental stage your child is at, there is hope for a bright future. The case studies presented in the previous chapter show that whenever the diagnosis occurs, treatment plans can be implemented that can help your child overcome even years of suffering with this disruptive behavioral disorder.

The goal of this book is to present you with a compassionate overview of ODD so that you can gain a more comprehensive understanding of this condition. Your child may not just be obstinate or independent; they may, in fact, be suffering from a behavioral disorder over which they have little control. Imagine being unable to control extreme emotions as they fill you with rage or despair. But, your child doesn't have to continue suffering from uncontrollable emotions. There is help. Start by documenting the behaviors you see and rule out any medical causes of disruptive behavior. From there, talk with a behavioral specialist about triggers you've identified and any problems your family might be experiencing.

If a diagnosis of ODD is made, now the healing can begin. There are a number of therapies that can help your child and your whole family to conquer this problem. You don't have to live in fear of the next tantrum or that your child may ruin their life with their disruptive behavior. There are effective treatments that can help turn things around no matter at what age a diagnosis is made. Don't be afraid to seek that help. You might just find out that your child's diagnosis can help you resolve some of your own issues as well.

There are a number of helpful resources if you find that your child has ODD. Check out some of the websites listed here:

Websites

- Lives in the Balance is a website which helps assist children through the use of collaborative problem-solving.
- Transforming the Difficult Child utilizes different ways to help children manage their intense emotions.
- Teens with Problems is designed especially for teens and covers an array of problems including ODD.
- American Academy of Child & Adult Psychiatry provides more information related to ODD as well as resources for getting help.
- Cincinnati Children's Hospital Medical Center also has some great information about ODD and helpful resources.

Whatever you do, don't give up. Your child needs you, and you can help. Start by implementing some of the tips in this book to begin healing today.

REFERENCES

Bada, H. S., Das, A., Bauer, C. R., Shankaran, S., Lester, B., LaGasse, L., Hammond, J., Wright, L. L., & Higgins, R. (2007). Impact of Prenatal Cocaine Exposure on Child Behavior Problems Through School Age. PEDIATRICS, 119(2), e348–e359. https://doi.org/10.1542/peds.2006-1404

Biederman J, Faraone S, Milberger S, Guite J, Mick E, Chen L, et al. (1996). A prospective 4- year follow-up study of attention-deficit hyperactivity and related disorders. Archives of General Psychiatry; 53(5):437-46.

Biederman J, Faraone S, Mick E, Lelon E. (1995). Psychiatric comorbidity among referred ju – veniles with major depression: fact or artifact? Journal of the American Academy of Child and Adolescent Psychiatry; 34(5):579-90.

Chen M-H, Su T-P, Chen Y-S, Hsu J-W, Huang K-L, Chang W-H, et al. (2013). Higher risk of developing mood disorders among adolescents with comorbidity of attention deficit hyperactivity disorder and disruptive behavior disorder: a nationwide prospective study. Journal of Psychiatric Research; 47(8):1019-23.

de Zeeuw, E. L., van Beijsterveldt, C. E. M., Lubke, G. H., Glasner, T. J., & Boomsma, D. I. (2015). Childhood ODD and ADHD Behavior: The Effect of Classroom Sharing, Gender, Teacher Gender and Their Interactions. Behavior Genetics, 45(4), 394–408. https://doi.org/10.1007/s10519-015-9712-z

Dix, T., Stewart, A. D., Gershoff, E. T., & Day, W. H. (2007). Autonomy and Children?s Reactions to Being Controlled: Evidence That Both Compliance and Defiance May Be Positive Markers in Early Development. Child Development, 78(4), 1204–1221. https://doi.org/10.1111/j.1467-8624.2007.01061.x

Drabick, D. A. G., Gadow, K. D., & Loney, J. (2008). Co-Occurring ODD and GAD Symptom Groups: Source-Specific Syndromes and Cross-Informant Comorbidity. Journal of Clinical Child & Adolescent Psychology, 37(2), 314–326. https://doi.org/10.1080/15374410801955862

Ghosh, S., & Sinha, M. (2012). ADHD, ODD, and CD: Do They Belong to a Common Psychopathological Spectrum? A Case Series. Case Reports in Psychiatry, 2012, 1–4. https://doi.org/10.1155/2012/520689

Gump, B. B., Dykas, M. J., MacKenzie, J. A., Dumas, A. K., Hruska, B., Ewart, C. K., Parsons, P. J., Palmer, C. D., & Bendinskas, K. (2017). Background lead and mercury exposures: Psychological and behavioral problems in children. Environmental Research, 158, 576–582. https://doi.org/10.1016/j.envres.2017.06.033

Jacobs, R. H., Becker-Weidman, E. G., Reinecke, M. A., Jordan, N., Silva, S. G., Rohde, P., & March, J. S. (2010). Treating Depression and Oppositional Behavior in Adolescents. Journal of Clinical Child & Adolescent Psychology, 39(4), 559–567. https://doi.org/10.1080/15374416.2010.486318

Joshi, G., & Wilens, T. (2009). Comorbidity in Pediatric Bipolar Disorder. Child and Adolescent Psychiatric Clinics of North America, 18(2), 291–319. https://doi.org/10.1016/j.chc.2008.12.005

Linares, T. J., Singer, L. T., Kirchner, H. L., Short, E. J., Min, M. O., Hussey, P., & Minnes, S. (2005). Mental Health Outcomes of Cocaine-Exposed Children at 6 Years of Age. *Journal of Pediatric Psychology, 31*(1), 85–97. https://doi.org/10.1093/jpepsy/jsj020

Matlock, J, and Green, V. (1990). The effects of day care on the social and emotional development of infants, toddlers, and preschoolers. *Early Child Development and Care, 64*, 55-59.

McGee, R., & Williams, S. (1999). Environmental Risk Factors in Oppositional-Defiant Disorder and Conduct Disorder. *Handbook of Disruptive Behavior Disorders*, 419–440. https://doi.org/10.1007/978-1-4615-4881-2_19

Mikolajewski, A. J., Taylor, J., & Iacono, W. G. (2017). Oppositional defiant disorder dimensions: genetic influences and risk for later psychopathology. *Journal of Child Psychology and Psychiatry, 58*(6), 702–710. https://doi.org/10.1111/jcpp.12683

Rodgers, S., Müller, M., Rössler, W., Castelao, E., Preisig, M., & Ajdacic-Gross, V. (2014). Externalizing disorders and substance use: empirically derived subtypes in a population-based sample of adults. *Social Psychiatry and Psychiatric Epidemiology, 50*(1), 7–17. https://doi.org/10.1007/s00127-014-0898-9

Russell, A. A., Johnson, C. L., Hammad, A., Ristau, K. I., Zawadzki, S., Del Alba Villar, L., & Coker, K. L. (2015). Prenatal and Neighborhood Correlates of Oppositional Defiant Disorder (ODD). *Child and Adolescent Social Work Journal, 32*(4), 375–381. https://doi.org/10.1007/s10560-015-0379-3

Saarinen S, Fontell T, Vuontela V, Carlson S, Aronen ET. (2014). Visuospatial working memory in 7-to 12-year-old children with disruptive behavior disorders. *Child Psychiatry and Human Development*; 1-10.
Spears, G. V., Stein, J. A., & Koniak-Griffin, D. (2010). Latent growth trajectories of substance use among pregnant and parenting adolescents.

Psychology of Addictive Behaviors, 24(2), 322–332. https://doi.org/10. 1037/a0018518

[20] Thapar A, Harrington R, McGUFFIN P. (2001). Examining the comorbidity of ADHD-relat – ed behaviours and conduct problems using a twin study design. British Journal of Psychiatry;179(3):224-9. [21]

Printed in Great Britain
by Amazon